MW00529519

12

Steps to an
Addictive Free
Life

AFL

12

Steps to an
Addictive Free
Life

Revised Edition

ANTHONY ORDILLE

12 Steps to an Addictive Free Life
Copyright © 2016 by Anthony Ordille. All rights reserved.

No part of this publication may be reproduced, stored in a retrieval system or transmitted in any way by any means, electronic, mechanical, photocopy, recording or otherwise without the prior permission of the author except as provided by USA copyright law.

Scripture quotations marked (AMP) are taken from the *Amplified Bible*, Copyright © 1954, 1958, 1962, 1964, 1965, 1987 by The Lockman Foundation. Used by permission.

Scripture quotations marked (ASV) are taken from the *American Standard Version*, Thomas Nelson & Sons, 1901. Used by permission. All rights reserved.

Scripture quotations marked (ESV) are from *The Holy Bible, English Standard Version®*, copyright © 2001 by Crossway Bibles, a publishing ministry of Good News Publishers. Used by permission. All rights reserved.

Scripture quotations marked (MSG) are taken from *The Message*. Copyright © 1993, 1994, 1995, 1996, 2000, 2001, 2002. Used by permission of NavPress Publishing Group.

Scripture quotations marked (NIV) are taken from the *Holy Bible, New International Version®*, NIV®. Copyright © 1973, 1978, 1984 by Biblica, Inc.™ Used by permission of Zondervan. All rights reserved worldwide. www.zondervan.com

Scripture quotations marked (NLT) are taken from the Holy Bible, New Living Translation, copyright 1996, 2004, 2007, 2015 by Tyndale House Foundation. Used by permission of Tyndale House Publishers, Inc., Carol Stream, Illinois 60188. All rights reserved.

Unless otherwise noted, all scripture is from the New King James Version of the Bible. Copyright © 1982 by Thomas Nelson, Inc. Used by permission. All rights reserved.

This book is designed to provide accurate and authoritative information with regard to the subject matter covered. This information is given with the understanding that neither the author nor any associate of AFL is engaged in rendering legal, professional advice. Since the details of your situation are fact dependent, you should additionally seek the services of a competent professional.

www.anthonyordille.com
Cover design by Norlan Balazo
Interior design by Shieldon Alcasid
Book Layout © 2017 BookDesignTemplates.com

Published in the United States of America

ISBN: 978-1-68270-118-8 (1st Edition, Published 2016)
ISBN: 978-0-99962-771-6 (Revised Edition, Published 2017)
ISBN: 978-0-99962-773-0 (eBook)
ISBN: 978-0-99962-774-7 (Hardcover)

Self-Help / Substance Abuse & Addictions / General
Self-Help / Twelve-Step Programs
Religion / Christian Ministry / Counseling & Recovery
12.22

Acknowledgments

Special thanks to the following people:

Reed & Reed Consulting
Renee Ordille
Jarred Ordille
Dale Hinz
Zach Neese
Crystal Maria Scott
Beverly Engel
Ps. Tim Ross

To all those who have turned in a testimony,
Thank you!

Contents

Mission Statement

Our mission is to reach out to the hurting, give encouragement to the weak and extend hope to the lost. To share the truth about the living word of God and give hope to those who are struggling with addictions of all kinds. To let them know they can recover through deliverance and live a life of freedom from this crippling disease.

We are called to reveal the mysteries of God's word from his word according to Matthew 13:11.

To proclaim the love of God to all the world, and that he walked on this earth as a man by the name of Jesus. (Luke 2:11)

To proclaim that Jesus Is Lord, from the top of the world to the bottom, and all the way around, and to show that he is the only way to heaven. (John 10:1, 14:6, Hebrews 10:20)

We want to help people know who they are in Christ and what the will of God is for their lives. (Psalms 118:8)

Our vision is to see restoration of the hurt and dying in this world. To help the lost find a place of rest so they can learn how to cope with life in general, through love and the help of the Holy Spirit. To be built up in all that God has for them so they too can proclaim the works of the Lord.

Introduction

This guidebook was written with the hope that it will help those who are struggling with addictions and to show that there is a way out. It is designed to help those struggling with addictions of all kinds. The only difference between addicts is the choice of addiction, but in most cases, the mind-set runs the same path. Most addicts are directed to the traditional twelve-step program, but for those who want to lean on the truth about God, there is another way to an Addictive Free Life.

We want you to know that you are loved by so many people who are willing to love you until you can love yourself, and the only thing you need to do is show up. All of us who have walked this out before you are cheering you on and hoping that you will read and put to work this guidebook so that one day you can share with others your freedom.

AFL will show you that way! As long as you keep the faith and follow the direction given, you stand a great chance to beat the addiction that holds you captive. One of the clichés we believe to be true is "You cannot do this alone!" That is found in almost every recovery program known to mankind.

The author has been where you are and has seen firsthand the recovery through the traditional way and now lives his life in freedom from this crippling disease, because he has found what you are about to find. You will be able to read his testimony in the back of the book.

Today you have a choice to make: You can stay where you are and continue to live in your pain, sickness, disease, and the path to destruction, which leads to death. Or you can go through life in a recovery program with the hope that you will never use again. Or you can accept God's way and live your life free of the addiction. It is your willingness to know the difference between what is right and what is wrong. God will change your life if you let Him. If you open your heart and your mind as you go through these chapters and steps, He will meet you right where you are.

The guidebook layout suggests reading first each chapter in section 1 before making any decisions. After reading each chapter and deciding you want the challenge, work the steps in chapter 4 from step 1 to step 12. We have designed a workbook that you may find helpful when you start. Use the back sections as references and use the scriptures in your daily living.

Unlike the traditional twelve-step programs, AFL is a Christ-centered fellowship that focuses on the word of God with a relationship with his son. Because after all, Jesus came to set the captives free (Jeremiah 29:14). Addiction is a form of captivity, isn't it? You have become enslaved to the stronghold that keeps you bound together with the addiction. You are a prisoner to this way of life, and you need to learn how-to walk-in freedom.

12 Steps to an Addictive Free Life will bring out the best of who you really are. It will help you to grow in your faith, to learn God's word, to be an overcomer, and to walk over the hurdles that are in your way. Most importantly, it will help you realize that just because you have made some mistakes, you are not doomed for nonexistence in this society.

You are about to embark on a journey you may not care for. Unfortunately, not everyone will take this journey to the very end. Some of you may totally disagree about what is presented in this guidebook; therefore you will not receive what it has to offer. Some of you are so sick and tired of fighting the addiction that you are about ready to do anything to get rid of it. In this case, you will have to be totally open -minded and you will have to allow the work of the Lord to change your life. For those of you who will have a hard time accepting this guidebook, we hope by the time you finish reading it, you will have a change of heart. You will be reading a lot of scriptures because it is the word of God penetrating into the human spirit that will help and guide and change every situation. When his word is spoken out loud, it creates what it says; so when you get to some of the scriptures, you will need to speak them—not just read them but speak them out! The bottom line of this journey you are about to take; it is like anything else in this world. You have to apply the wisdom and the knowledge into your situation, and you have to work at the change. Change does not come without applying what you have learned.

You are beautiful and worth more than any addiction has to offer. You are a treasure waiting to be discovered so the beauty that God made you to be will shine!

You are about to embark on the road to freedom!

Welcome!

Section 1

An Addictive Free Life! (AFL)

Chapters 1-9

The following chapters will change your life!
If you let it!

Chapter 1

Do I Belong Here?

Where is here? Here is anywhere you are seeking help. It may be a one-on-one session with a pastor, counselor, psychiatrist, parent, or leadership in the church. It may be a small house group, or it may be a large meeting. Here is anywhere that is going to help you understand that you have a problem, and you need help. Help is not found by people who are still active in their addiction. All of those mentioned above are a great source, but the true people who can help are the ones that have gone through the pain that addiction brings and overcame it. Jesus has gone through the pain when he walked this earth for thirty -three years— not as an addict like us, but as someone who knows what it feels like to suffer and the urge to give up. That is why the Bible is a great source and the backbone of AFL.

In the gospels Matthew, Mark, Luke, and John talk about the time Jesus was in ministry and all he went through during those three and one -half years. What you might not see is that during the first thirty-something odd years before his ministry started, he was a normal child with all the same feelings, hurts, and pain we all went through as a child, and some of us are still going through them today.

He was a carpenter's son (Matthew 13:55) and most likely was taught by his earthly father, Joseph, how to build things out of wood and use a saw and a hammer. Do you think he ever smashed his thumb or maybe got cut using the saw? The author is a carpenter and knows in the years of working in this field he has smashed his thumb swinging a hammer on a number of occasions. He has cut himself from a saw a time or two. Each time it has caused him pain. So if we feel pain, Jesus felt pain too when he was in a body. Jesus was a boy, and like most little boys, he most likely enjoyed running and climbing trees, which we are certain he would have needed some TLC from his mother, Mary.

How about the time his parents went to Jerusalem for the Passover feast, and when it was over, Mary and Joseph left without him? Jesus was twelve years old that year, and just maybe, for a second, he felt what it was like to be abandoned by his parents. On the cross, just before he died, he felt the most severe pain unimaginable. It was a harsh death to begin with, and then seconds before he died, he felt all the sins of the world at one time, and that is why he said, "My God, my God, why have you forsaken me?" (Matthew 27:46). It must have been the most unbearable pain anyone could take. How about God's pain having to watch his only son die hanging on the cross with nails through the hands and feet? One last thing on this matter: Jesus was God who left his place in heaven to come to earth to save us. He had to take on a human body to legally have a right to be here.

Humans are all the same, but our spirits are different. We all have feelings; we all hurt inside because of those feelings. Our bodies feel pain when our flesh is cut or have nails driven through them. This is why we believe that Jesus felt the same pain we all go through.

In the gospel of Luke, chapter 22, it explains the last supper that most of us are aware of, but what you might not know is after the supper he was walking with his disciples. Verses 40–44 goes like this in the Amplified Bible:

And when he came to the place, he said to them, pray that you may not [at all] enter into temptation. And he withdrew from them about a stone's throw and knelt down and prayed, saying Father, if you are willing, remove this cup from me; yet not my will, but [always] yours be done. And there appeared to him an angel from heaven, strengthening him in spirit. And being in an agony [of mind], he prayed [all the] more earnestly and intently, and sweat became like great clots of blood dropping down upon the ground.

If that is not someone who understands pain and looking for a way out, we do not know who is. Jesus turned to a power greater than himself to remove the pain, but he never gave up on doing what was right. Do you ever feel like your pain is so great that you just want to give up? Has your pain ever been so great that you think you are the only one going through that situation? Know that you are not alone, and you have to seek help from heaven to strengthen your spirit just like the angel did for Jesus. That is what here is all about!

Even though you will find guidance from someone here on earth, you will have to draw the strength needed to put the addiction behind you from heaven. There are a lot of good programs out there that will help you stop the addiction, but the only way to ever have a chance at walking this out in freedom is turning your will and life over to the care of God, not just as a higher power of your own understanding. That is why the next chapters and steps will change your life if you focus on the things above and not on the things of this earth (Colossians 3:2).

Now please understand, you still need to turn to man for answers just like a baby has to count on their parents to take care of them. One day you can feed on the word for yourself and not have to lean on man as much, but until then, keep in the program. In 1 Corinthians 3:2, the Amplified Bible says it this way: *"I fed you with milk, not solid food, for you were not yet strong enough [to be ready for it]; but even yet you are not strong enough [to be ready for it]."* Please note that you will always need someone to be accountable to, and you will never be able to do it alone.

This guidebook can be your lifeline and was written just for you. AFL will never judge you or condemn you for being different. The only thing we care about is you, and that you want to care about yourself.

Ask yourself,

Do I belong here?

Now in order for you to answer this question, let us start off with a meaning for addiction from the *Merriam-Webster's Collegiate Dictionary.*[1]

: the quality or state of being addicted; addiction to reading.
: compulsive need for and use of a habit-forming substance (as heroin, nicotine, or alcohol) characterized by tolerance and by well-defined physiological symptoms upon withdrawal; broadly: persistent compulsive use of a substance known by the user to be harmful.

Addictions are not limited to alcohol abuse and drug abuse. They can be behavior addiction, as in exercise abuse, overeating, pornography, and gambling. The classic hallmarks of addiction include impaired control over substances, behavior, giving full attention to the substance or behavior, continued use despite consequences, and denial, no matter how hard one tries to stop. Habits and patterns associated with addiction are typically characterized by immediate gratification (otherwise known as short-term reward) coupled with delayed harmful effects, which leans toward long-term costs.

Physiological dependence occurs when the body has to adjust to the substance/behavior by combining the substance/behavior into its "normal" functioning. This state creates the conditions of tolerance and withdrawal. Tolerance is the process by which the body continually adapts to the substance/behavior and requires increasingly larger amounts to achieve the original effects. This process starts right from the beginning. That is why it is so ludicrous that people say smoking marijuana has no effect on our bodies. Withdrawal refers to physical and psychological symptoms people experience when reducing or discontinuing a substance the body had become dependent on. This does not exclude behavior addictions.

Some of the symptoms of withdrawal generally include anxiety, irritability, intense cravings for the substance, nausea, hallucinations, headaches, cold sweats, and tremors, just to name a few.

As you can see, this term does not just mean a person who is on drugs or alcohol; it can be someone who has an eating disorder, a gambling habit, lying obsession—basically anyone who does things they do not want to do can be symptoms of an addiction. You try to will yourself to stop, but you cannot. Maybe it has gotten to the point you do not even know right from wrong. How about the meaning of addict?

The *Webster's Dictionary of the English Language*[2] says it is

1. a person who is addicted: a drug addict (v. t.);
2. to .give (oneself) up to something habitually;
3. to cause (a person) to depend physiologically on a drug.

The *Merriam-Webster's Collegiate Dictionary*[3] puts it this way:

1. to devote or surrender (oneself) to something habitually or obsessively <addicted to gambling.
2. to cause addiction to a substance in (a person or animal).

Very simply put, it is any mind-altering, mood-changing substance or habit that causes a problem in any area of your life. So, are you struggling with something that you do not want in your life? If the answer is yes, you may belong here.

People with illicit addictions may enjoy the secretive nature of their behavior. They may blame society for its narrow-mindedness, choosing to see themselves as freewill and independent individuals. In reality, addictions tend to limit people's individuality and freedom as they become more restricted in their behaviors. Imprisonment for engaging in an illegal addiction restricts their freedom even more.

Even though the word addict may be used throughout this guidebook, you can reference it to the type of problem you are dealing with. Please note, an addict is anyone who is struggling with an addiction that controls his or her life; it does not have to be a drug.

How does one know that they have a drug problem, an alcohol problem, a gambling problem, overeating problem, a lying spirit, or any other addictive behaviors? Asking those people around you are one of the ways. Taking an inventory of your life can be a remarkably effective way. Look at the people you are hanging out with is a great practice. There are all kinds of programs that can answer this question, and you can Google and find hundreds of helpful websites, but here are some basic questions that we compiled, and we call this the *"How well do I know myself"* test.

Be Honest with your answers so you have a truthful diagnosis. You can also find this in the workbook.

- Can you control your habit? Yes/No

- Have you ever forgotten where you were, what you were doing, and how you got home (FYI, this is called a blackout)? Yes/No

- Do you put the addiction above your family, friends, or job? Yes/No

- Do you steal to pay for your habit? Yes/No

- Will you keep going even when you know you should stop? Yes/No

- Do you lie about it to others? Yes/No Do you dream about it? Yes/No

- Have you ever been in jail because of it? Yes/No Are you antisocial? Yes/No

- Are you emotionally bankrupt? Yes/No

- Are you destructive? Yes/No

- Have you ever felt dying would be better than living? Yes/No

- Does the addiction soothe the pain? Yes/No

- Do you find it hard to tell the truth? Yes/No

- Have you gone into debt because you think the next game will be the big one? Yes/No

- On the drug and alcohol side, do you remember what you did last night? Yes/No

- Do you remember how the show you were watching ended? Yes/No

- Do you remember how you got home from the bar last night? Yes/No

- Do you remember who you were with last night? Yes/No

- Do you remember the conversation you had with your wife/husband or children when you got home from work yesterday after you stopped at the bar for just a drink? Yes/No

- Do you get hostile? Yes/No

- Do you know you have a problem but think you can do it by yourself? Yes/No

- Do you find yourself throwing pity parties? Yes/No

These are all signs that you do belong here. We are not going to put a score on this questionnaire because only you can score yourself. We would say that one yes can mean that you have an addiction problem, but only you can answer this right, and only you have the ability to make the right choice. Only you can take the first step toward freedom.

Are you willing?

Do not live-in denial anymore; be honest with yourself... even if it is for the very first time. You do not need to carry this alone, and that is what AFL is all about.

Everyone is addicted to something, but not everyone has a problem with addiction. If you think you have a problem, then keep reading. If not, then keep reading anyway; you just might learn something new. And then make sure to pass this guidebook on to someone who will use it; it just might change their life.

Chapter 2

Is There Hope for Me?

If you are seeking for answers because you are tired of being sick and tired of dealing with the addiction, then you are in the right place. Do not let the inability to cope with daily life get you down to the point that you feel there is no return. There is always hope when you get into the right place.

- ✓ A place that will show you how to live your life free from the addiction!
- ✓ A place that will show you how to love yourself then how to love others!
- ✓ A place that will show how to think differently!
- ✓ A place like no other. It is called a little bit of heaven on earth; we call this place the throne room of God. The only way to get there is by believing in his word and allowing your spirit to be coupled with his.

AFL wants to show you through this guidebook, and/ or meetings, that such a place exists, and that the door is always open. We will model after it and every time we come together; we will reveal it.

Now let us shed some more light about addiction. Whether you are a drug addict or addicted to some other type of addiction, it all works the same. Addiction is not hereditary; addiction is a seed that is planted in one's life by curses, images, and a variety of open doors. You are not an addict hooked on drugs because your ancestors were alcoholics or maybe Uncle Clyde shot heroin. You may have seen Uncle Clyde high and out of control, or maybe you saw your mom or dad drunk all the time stumbling around the house. That is called a seed being planted in one's mind. That was an image that played over and over again in your subconscious. We have a lot of TV programs, movies, and other media that give us these images. In a basic sense it is glorifying what is really wrong. You have a problem with addiction because that seed was planted in your life as a curse, either by someone in your past or starting with you as a baby.

Here is an example of a seed being planted without knowing: A little baby sitting in a room with mom and dad as they are smoking a joint. The room gets filled with smoke as the baby is breathing it in. Now let us advance sixteen years; Mom and Dad wonder why their little baby, who now is sixteen years old, is smoking marijuana (or maybe something worse) even if they themselves have not smoked it for years.

So to clarify some of the misconceptions that were told to you—that you are an alcoholic, drug addict, gambler, or any other name, because it is in your bloodline or you have an eating problem because it is in the DNA of your family—we are here to tell you, that statement is incorrect in spite of what so many studies have shown. The word of God is over all! It is the seed that was planted that caused a reaction, a growth. It is no different than if you took an apple seed and planted it in the ground, you will get an apple tree. You cannot expect to plant an apple seed and get an orange tree. There is only one way to kill that seed, even if it grows into a ripe, fully blossomed, fruit-producing tree. You can stand on the word of God and with your mouth, curse it right out of your life and then allowing it to dry up and wither, to never produce another year, month, week, day, even a moment of being addicted to the addiction.

We have a testimony in section 2 from a man who struggled with a lie about who he was. When he was sexually abused as a young child, it started a chain reaction of consequences. First was protecting the secret. Next came an addiction to pornography. That was followed by living a double life. At age nineteen, the secret was exposed, and with it came freedom. Was he born destined to be addicted to porn? Absolutely not! There was a seed planted in his bloodline that was allowed to take root until one day, he got a hold of the truth and cursed it. Tim's experience shows how the love of Christ can win out— and the love of people can help change how one lives a life. [1]

Many would say that addictions are incurable; there are hundreds of scriptures that prove otherwise. The only reason we can think why they would say this is they do not want to believe in the true living deity who is greater than themselves. The Bible says that Jesus has healed all of those who believe.

> *And Jesus went about all Galilee, teaching in their synagogues, preaching the gospel of the kingdom, and healing all kinds of sickness and all kinds of disease among the people. (Matthew 4:23)*

> *But he was wounded for our transgressions, he was bruised for our iniquities; the chastisement of our peace was upon him; and with his stripes we are healed. (Isaiah 53:5, ASV)*

> *Confess your trespasses to one another, and pray for one another, that you may be healed. The effective, fervent prayer of a righteous man avails much. (James 5:16)*

There are so many other scriptures that confess healing. We cannot list them all, but here are just a few to make the point. If you would like to read more of them, go look up *healing, healed, heals* in a Bible concordance.

> *And when the sun was setting, all they that had any sick with divers diseases brought them unto him; and he laid his hands on every one of them, and healed them.* (Luke 4:40, ASV)

> *But so much the more went abroad the report concerning him: and great multitudes came together to hear, and to be healed of their infirmities.* (Luke 5:15, ASV)

> *And a woman having an issue of blood twelve years, who had spent all her living upon physicians, and could not be healed of any.* (Luke 8:43, ASV)

> *Who his own self bare our sins in his body upon the tree, that we, having died unto sins, might live unto righteousness; by whose stripes ye were healed.* (1 Peter 2:24, ASV)

> *O Jehovah my God, I cried unto thee, and thou hast healed me.* (Psalm 30:2, ASV)

> *He sent his word, and healed them, and delivered them from their destructions.* (Psalm 107:20)

> *Heal me, O Lord, and I shall be healed; save me, and I shall be saved: for thou art my praise.* (Jeremiah 17:14)

Can you see with these few scriptures how much God wants to heal you? Although you may feel physically or mentally drained, there is hope. When a person does not give up, it allows the Lord to move in their life. Allowing the Holy Spirit to come into a person's spirit will rejuvenate one's soul. This starts the healing process both inside and out. When you never give up hope, you allow yourselves time to adjust your course and get back on the right path.

Here are a few scriptures to get started with:

Be strong, and let your heart take courage, All ye that hope in Jehovah. (Psalm 31:24, ASV)

Behold, the eye of Jehovah is upon them that fear him, Upon them that hope in his lovingkindness. (Psalm 33:18, ASV)

For in thee, O Jehovah, do I hope: Thou wilt answer, O Lord my God. (Psalms 38:15, ASV)

Hope deferred makes the heart sick, But when the desire comes, it is a tree of life. (Proverbs 13:12)

The wicked is banished in his wickedness, but the righteous has hope in his death. (Proverbs 14:32)

I'll never forget the trouble, the utter lostness, the taste of ashes, the poison I've swallowed. I remember it all— oh, how well I remember— the feeling of hitting the bottom. But there's one other thing I remember, and remembering, I keep a grip on hope. (Lamentations 3:19–21, MSG)

The bottom line to this whole controversy that addictions are incurable is that there is nothing in this world that is not God's or is not put under his feet. "For, He has put all things under His feet.*" But when He says "all things are put under Him," it is evident that He who put all things under Him is excepted"* (1 Corinthians 15:27). If you believe the addiction is under his feet, you will walk in victory; and no one can change that, not even the devil himself.

When you have hope, it offers more than the addiction. If you walk around all day with the hope of glory on your mind and in your heart, you do not leave enough room for the addiction to take root anymore. Is this easy to do? Of course not. When you live in a world of temptations all around you, you can fall short. That is why you have to pick yourself up and keep company with like people, folks that will be there to hold on to you and tell you where you went wrong. Of course, you have to be willing to allow them into your world and become transparent to them. If you want them to know you are hurting, you need to tell them!

In other programs, they will tell you that you will have to keep going back until the day you die. The author and so many others are proven testimonies that it is just not so. You will, however, have to keep coming back not to get a reward from man but to learn how to seek God and walk in his ways. Just like a newborn has to depend on their parents to wash and feed them, change their diapers, rock them to sleep. You will need to be nurtured until the time that you can be weaned off the milk. You will then learn how to feed for yourself and show others to do the same thing. At that point you will only need to attend meetings for yourself about 1 percent of the time and 99 percent for others. When you give of yourself, there is no time for the addiction to take root. This is how you will grow and earn a medal of honor from your Lord rather than from man.

AFL will not be giving out medals to reward your time here; we will only be giving out hugs and words of encouragement. There are testimonies in the back of the guidebook from others who have gone through the same course of action and now live their life free from addictions. These testimonies will grow because of the word of God and will be added to future printings and the website. Remember that this is an ongoing process, just not in a recovery standpoint. Of course, you can fall if you step out from under the covering of the Almighty, but God has made a way for you to get back, and you do not need to start all over again earning rewards. He will forgive you and put you right back on course. You will learn more about this when you get to chapter 6.

Freedom from addictions is not hopeless, living in bondage is! You have to be willing to walk away from your current lifestyle and learn how to be clean, set free from stinking thinking, and to fall in love with yourself. You have to have the desperation to come out from the addiction to a new way of living. After you start this, the hope just keeps building until you have a great wall behind you that no devil can get to you. Your future will be wide open for you to walk in, and the skies will be clearer. Just knowing that you are never alone can ease the pain.

We are so proud of you for making it this far that it blesses our souls. It would be a great triumph to have all who are hurting make it this far, so you have made a great step into your deliverance. We are hopeful that as you continue on to the other chapters, you will start to grow and then you are on your way to a newfound love...*yourself!*

You can use the workbook to write down your own statement of hope and to see yourself freed from the addiction.

Chapter 3

Stepping into Faith!

In order for you to continue, we need to make sure you understand a few things. In order for you to be set free, healed, and delivered by working the twelve steps in the next chapter, you have to make a decision first. It was mentioned in the introduction that this is unlike other recovery programs where they make mention that they are not about religion. We are not about religion either, but we are about God and the truth of the written word. We are about letting the Holy Spirit rule and reign in our lives. We believe that the Bible is the infallible word from God, written by the inspiration from the Holy Spirit, given to us in hopes that all who read it will be children of God.

You must become a child of God in order for the blessing to work and the doors of heaven to be open to all that you need. You will be given the opportunity to do this in step 3. You must know how it feels to be loved by the Father, even if you have one here on earth, and you can only obtain this from the scriptures. You cannot learn this love unless you know love himself. God is the greatest love known to mankind; it is called *agape*. You will find it throughout the Bible, and there is no denying its existence.

Agape is selfless, sacrificial, unconditional love, and it is the highest love you will ever know. Jesus was the greatest example of this love when he gave of himself on the cross. You can see it in the greatest known scripture quoted, John 3:16; *"For God so loved the world that he gave of his only son, so that whoever believes in him shall not perish but have eternal life."* God gave his only son for you. Did you hear that? He gave just for you! If you were asked to sacrifice your child to save the world, would you do it? It would be extremely hard for you to decide, unless you trusted that your child would be raised up from the dead. That is what love does; it takes what is dead and raises it up to a new life. That is what 1 Corinthians 6:14 says, *"And God both raised up the Lord and will also raise us up by His power."*

Agape is a Greek word, and variations of it are found throughout the New Testament. Agape perfectly describes the kind of love Jesus Christ has for his Father and for his followers: *"Whoever has my commands and keeps them is the one who loves me. The one who loves me will be loved by my Father, and I too will love them and show myself to them"* (John 14:21, NIV).

Jesus lived out agape by sacrificing himself for the sins of the world. *"And He Himself is the propitiation for our sins, and not for ours only but also for the whole world"* (1 John 2:2). Do you have a friend like that here on earth? One like in John 15:13: *"Greater love has no one than this: than to lay down one's life for friends"*

This is why it is so important for you to know the Father from above. He is the only way you will overcome the addiction. You will need to follow Jesus's example and lay down your life to him, along with the addiction, so he can pick it back up as a new creation. This is how it is seen in 2 Corinthians 5:17: *"Therefore, if anyone is in Christ, he is a new creation; old things have passed away; behold, all things have become new."*

If you no longer have the addiction, you will no longer be the person you know right now. You will be the person you were born to be. So if you are struggling with an addiction of any kind or sickness in your body, know that God wants to heal you and set you free, but this can only be done by faith and the grace of God. You have to see yourself free, clean, and living differently from the lifestyle with addiction before it can manifest into what is real to you.

Faith works sometimes in your life just because you believe that God's word is alive. One time the author of this guidebook went on a twenty-eight-day fast for our nation and had no desire to go back drinking coffee when it was over. Another time before that, he went to a healing service at a church and walked out not desiring cigarettes. So God's power works in every addiction we are struggling with, not just the hard cases.

Faith believes in what is true. There are two elements that can make up faith: First it is being convinced of the truth and being certain of reality, having evidence of unseen things. The second element is believing, hoping, embracing, and seizing the truth. While faith requires being convinced that what we believe in is true, just knowing the truth is only half of faith. To have faith work, you must believe!

Believing is not exactly the same as faith. For belief to be faith, it must illuminate on what is certainly true. Belief comes before seeing! Let us use an example on what we mean: Lets say a friend of yours from the other side of the country flies in to see you. As you are sitting at the table talking, they turn to you and say they came to give you their fully restored Mercedes. You jump up with excitement and ask where it is. They say to you that it was being shipped to you and hand you an envelope with the title. You open it up with the thrill that you are now the owner of something you cannot see, but you are believing in what they said about it being shipped to you is true. It is the same basis for believing in God. We cannot see him, yet he has given us a gift for salvation of life. That same intense excitement you would feel for the car should be the same belief in God because the title is the Bible. We can see the writings, we just have to believe that it is attached to what it says it is, just like the title to the car is just a piece of paper—but because of what it says, it makes you the owner.

You may be asking yourself how much faith you need. You only need enough faith to take the first step. If Moses did not take that first step into the water and stick his staff down into the wet ground, the water would have never parted, and the Israelites would have never been able to cross the Jordan. They would have been slaughtered by the Egyptians. He trusted God. He heard God's voice. God told him to take that path, so he trusted that God would get them to the other side. He believed what God told him, and he reacted.

Stop running around the mountain. You have to follow the path of God, which requires taking a leap of faith. When you take that first step, stay focused on Jesus. When Peter was called out of the boat to walk on the windswept Sea of Galilee toward Jesus, he took his eyes off Jesus, and he started to sink because fear of drowning came into his thought. The opposite of faith is fear. If you live in fear, you will never experience the potential that God has placed in you. Do not let fears of the unknown cripple your destiny. It is your destiny to be free from this addictive behavior.

We can see that scripture gives examples of situations where belief alone is required, even commanded. Just believe! Like Peter walking on the water—do not think, just act on what you hear! God requires us to believe in him because even when the evidence looks bad, he asks us to trust him. God requires belief and trust in moments of human weakness, but faith is what makes us strong. Faith is the state of being convinced about what we hope for.

You need the same faith that is found in the book of Hebrews 11:1: *"Now faith is the substance of things hoped for, the evidence of things not seen."* Chapter 11:6 says, "Because without faith, it is impossible to please God."

In 11:2—By faith, the men of old had divine testimony borne to them and obtained a good report.

In 11:3—By faith, we understand that the worlds were framed by the word of God, so that what we see was not made out of the things which are visible.

In 11:4—By faith, Abel brought God a better and more acceptable sacrifice than Cain.

In 11:5—Because of faith, Enoch was caught up in a whirlwind and transferred to heaven.

In 11:6—Because of our faith God is pleased with us.

In 11:7—By faith, Noah, being forewarned by God concerning events that had no visible sign, took heed to construct an ark.

In 11:8–10—By faith, Abraham, when he was called, obeyed, and went forth to a place which he was destined to receive as an inheritance and he went, although he did not know where he was to go.

In 11:11—Because of faith, Sarah herself received physical power to conceive a child, well past the age of conception, because she considered God who had given her the promise to be reliable and trustworthy and true to his word.

In 11:17—By faith, Abraham brought Isaac for an offering because he trusted that God would give him back because God told him before Isaac was conceived that through Isaac, he would be the father of all nations.

In 11:20—With eyes of faith, Isaac looking far into the future invoked blessings upon Jacob and Esau.

In 11:27—By faith, Moses led the Israelites out of Egypt and by faith they crossed the Red Sea as though on dry land.

In 11:30—By faith, the walls of Jericho fell down after they had been encompassed for seven days by the Israelites. Faith is calling those things that are not, as if they are, until they are.

Let us continue with the meaning of faith according to *Webster's New World Dictionary:*[1]

1. unquestioning belief that does not require proof or evidence,
2. unquestioning belief in God, religious tenets, etcetera,
3. a religion or a system of religious beliefs,
4. anything believed,
5. complete trust, confidence, or reliance,
6. allegiance to some person or thing: loyalty.

In Luke 17:5–6, the disciples were asking Jesus to increase their faith, and Jesus replied, *"If you have faith as small as a mustard seed, you can say to this mulberry tree, 'Be pulled up by the roots, and be planted in the sea,' and it will obey you."*

The Apostle Peter says it this way:

So brace up your minds; be sober (circumspect, morally alert); set your hope wholly and unchangeably on the grace (divine favor) that is coming to you when Jesus Christ (the Messiah) is revealed" (1 Peter 1:13, AMP).

Blessed be the God and Father of our Lord Jesus Christ, the Father of sympathy (pity and mercy) and the God [Who is the Source] of every comfort (consolation and encouragement), Who comforts (consoles and encourages) us in every trouble (calamity and affliction), so that we may also be able to comfort (console and encourage) those who are in any kind of trouble or distress, with the comfort (consolation and encouragement) with which we ourselves are comforted (consoled and encouraged) by God." (2 Corinthians 1:3–4, AMP).

After the account when Jesus was being tempted by the devil, in Luke chapter 4, he was teaching in the synagogue and was given the book of the prophet Isaiah where he read,

The Spirit of the Lord God is upon me, because the Lord has anointed and qualified me to preach the Gospel of good tidings to the meek, the poor, and afflicted; He has sent me to bind up and heal the brokenhearted, to proclaim liberty to the [physical and spiritual] captives and the opening of the prison and of the eyes to those who are bound, To proclaim the acceptable year of the Lord [the year of His favor] and the day of vengeance of our God, to comfort all who mourn. (Isaiah 61:1–2, AMP)

So faith is the builder of your future and opens up a decision that you will have to make and stick with. If you think that trying to stop the addiction on your own is hard, wait until you are confronted by your friends about your faith in God. The difference is, one is performed by you and the other is protected by God.

Faith does not come from trying harder; it comes from knowing God. The more you get to know God, because he is faithful, the better your faith becomes. The more you know him, the more you will trust his word. The way to trust him is to risk obeying him. The path of God is the most difficult, but when you fully surrender to it, it becomes the most rewarding. Having faith does not mean it is easy or that things will come quickly. Having faith is trusting God for all the right things at the right time. Sometimes you just have to be still, not a passive waiting around for something to happen, but a biblical waiting. Paul says that while we are waiting for God to set everything right, we suffer. But that suffering produces endurance; endurance produces character, and character produces hope. Hope itself is really a form of waiting.

Are you ready to put your faith in action? Are you ready to believe that what God did for others he will do for you? Are you willing to believe, even as small as a mustard seed, that God is who he says he is? And that he loves you? AFL is here for you to help you to grow in your faith, but you have to take the first steps. The next chapter is where you will build on the foundation of faith. We hope that you will read it through and then work the steps in numerical order so you will have peace, freedom, and a changed lifestyle.

Also for healing, you can read Isaiah 53:4–5, 58:8; Jeremiah 33:6; Matthew 4:23, 9:35; Luke 9:11, Acts 10:38 (only a few of the many places in the Bible that states that healing is for today). You can use the workbook to write down your statement of faith.

Chapter 4

Putting Your Faith into Action: Steps 1–12

So then Faith comes by hearing and hearing by the word
—Romans 10:17

If this is your first time reading this chapter, it is suggested that you finish reading section 1 of the guidebook before actually working the steps. We tell you this because we want you to have a full understanding of what AFL is all about and to help build up your faith.

If you are returning to work the steps, we hope that your faith has grown from hearing the word of God and you are ready to put the addiction behind you. When you are ready to put the addiction behind you, approach these steps with an open mind and an open heart so you can get the full benefit of this guidebook. Use the workbook as a tool to see yourself free. Ask God for the strength to be honest with yourself and to reveal any hidden secrets that can stop you. These steps are not about what we can do for you but what you can do for yourself. That is why it is the twelve "I haves" and not the twelve "we cans." Working them in order will give you the best outcome.

The Twelve "I Haves"

1.} I have come to the realization that addiction has ruled my life.

2.} I have acknowledged that God is the creator of all things.

3}. I have decided to confess salvation according to Romans 10:9–10.

4.} I have made a list of all my sins.

5.} I have repented with my mouth and asked forgiveness for each one of those sins.

6}. I have asked God for forgiveness and to remove any guilt or shame I put on myself.

7}. I have been delivered from all unrighteousness.

8}. I have asked God to show me all persons I have hurt and made a list.

9.} I have prayed over my hurt list seeking those I need to ask forgiveness from.

10} I have denied myself and will pick up my cross daily.

11} I have made a conscious decision to trust God and live a life of prayer.

12} I have found a body of believers to fellowship with and call my home.

This guidebook is for you to find a new identity. Up till now, you might have seen yourself, or even called yourself, an addict, glutton, gambler, sinner, but let it be known that is not how God sees you.

How do you see yourself?

Freedom begins now!

Are you sure you want to put the addiction behind you? This is not going to be easy at first. You will have to lay the old man down and renew your mind. You will have to spend time in the word of God, not just for the use of this guidebook. There will be times you will want to give up, but instead you will have to fall flat on your face and get into the presence of God. Remember, he is the only one that can set you free. No other name but the name of Jesus will override the urges. No twelve-step meetings no sponsor no religion nothing but him!

Thinking that you are any different than an alcoholic or a drug addict or a person who eats too much or a person who cannot stop gambling is not going to help you. No matter what the addiction is, the steps are the same. If you want to reach a chance of being free, you have to accept sin for what it is—*sin*! Of course, a person who is dealing with narcotics might not understand why a person, who has an eating disorder, cannot stop eating. And vice versa! But if you look beyond the addiction, you will see the same hurt, and that is what you can identify with. Addiction gives us a common ground for understanding one another.

When this guidebook was being constructed, one of the questions was, can people with different addictions be put under the same roof? If we look at the individual addiction, the answer would be no. But if we look at where the addiction started—a seed—the answer is yes.

Step 1

I have come to the realization that addiction has ruled my life

This is the most important step you will ever take. This is where the rubber meets the road, and you will need to come to grips with the stronghold. You are not reading this guidebook by mistake. If someone gave this guidebook to you, it is because they believe you need help. If you bought it, it is because you know you need help. The only other way you are reading this is you know the author and was curious on what he had to say. If the latter is the case, please pass this guidebook on to someone who can use help after you read it.

The addiction most likely has made you powerless over your will. You want to stop, but you cannot. You have tried to stop but had no success. When you look in a mirror, what do you see? If you are honest with this question, you will see someone who has lost control over their life and has fallen into a life of addiction. If you see someone who feels they are fine with the way their life is going, then you may be in denial. Denying the addiction will stop you from taking this step and giving yourself the greatest chance at a new life. You have to admit that there is a problem in order for you to overcome the addiction.

Are you happy with your life? Addictions can ruin a person's life, as well as their families. It can cause areas of your life to become unmanageable—jails, institutions, marriage issues, relationships, financial hardships, just to name a few. If you do not realize the fact that what you have been doing to yourself has put you on the wrong path, then you are in deeper than you think. You are heading for destruction with a false outlook.

You have to realize that your life is heading downward to a bottomless pit, and it is time to stop. You may feel as if you are too far down, and it looks as if the light above has faded away. We are here to assure you that the light is still there, and we can help you find it, but you need to take the first step just like Neil Armstrong said when he stepped off the ladder onto the moon, "That's one small step for man, one giant leap for mankind." You have to take one small step out of the addiction and one giant step into faith. Have faith in yourself that just for today you will not use, abuse, or want whatever it is that is holding you back. It does not matter how far down you have gone; what matters is that you are ready to climb back up!

Are you sick of being sick and tired? Are you tired of doing the things you no longer want to do but find yourself not being able to do the things you want to do? Addiction is progressive and can be fatal, no matter what the addiction is. It will dictate your path and how to walk that path. It will give false hope, make a lie seem like the truth, and tell you that everything is fine. It will make you believe that you do not have a problem; it is everyone else's fault. If you do not take a hold of it now, you may not have another chance. This is why AFL was formed: to speak the truth and tell you that if you keep going down the path you are on, you will end up in turmoil.

Step 1 means you have accepted that you have a problem and that you no longer desire to do unwanted behaviors again. This should be a big freedom for you; if not, you might want to check your pulse. Working this step means you are released from the chains that keep you bound to the addiction. You do not just say you come to the realization that addiction has ruled your life; you accept it and work at putting it behind you, one day at a time and sometimes just for this second. There is no magic to being delivered from an addictive lifestyle, but it does take faith in a power greater than you to work from the inside of your heart.

This may be the first time you have sought out help, or maybe you have gone through a twelve-step program without any results and you are saying to yourself, *Why should I believe that this time is going to be any different?* We cannot guarantee that this program will work for you, but we can guarantee that if you set forth the principles that are laid out in this guidebook and work them every day, you will have a better life! You have to see the good to uproot the bad.

We hope that you will not stop here but that you will take the next step of faith and go to step 2. We do not know what type of religion you come from, or if any at all, but if you really want to change your life and be set free from addictions, you will have to submit your life over to the person who created you. You will have to approach it with an open mind so it will go down deep inside your heart. Once your hardened heart becomes soft, you will have the best time of your life, guaranteed.

How do you see yourself?

On the road to freedom

!

Step 2

I have acknowledged that God is the creator of all things.

> *But without faith it is impossible to please Him, for he who comes to God must believe that He is, and that He is a rewarder of those who diligently seek Him.* (Hebrews 11:6)

One of the biggest downfalls to this step is the big bang theory and what our education system has taught—and still is teaching: that man has evolved from an ape. After reading the word of God with an open mind; there is no way that this could be true. With the complexity of how our bodies are made and how they function, it is extremely hard to believe that our ancestors were apes. Not with millions of people in the world all having different DNA and not one fingerprint being the same. Just look around and you can see God in everything. The color of the flowers, how creation lives and breathes, and the way nature takes care of itself. The depth of this subject is overwhelming and absorbing, so we will not spend too much time in it. The purpose of this step is for you to see and believe that God is the creator of your life and all you are and hopefully accept him.

Let us start with the history of Creation. It is no surprise that the first book of the Bible starts out with the creation of our universe and all that is in it. It is called the book of Genesis, the Greek word meaning "origin" or "beginning."

> *In the beginning God created the heavens and the earth. The earth was without form, and void; and darkness was on the face of the deep. And the Spirit of God was hovering over the face of the waters. Then God said,*

"Let there be light"; and there was light. And God saw the light, that it was good; and God divided the light from the darkness. God called the light Day, and the darkness He called Night. So the evening and the morning were the first day. Then God said, "Let there be a firmament in the midst of the waters, and let it divide the waters from the waters." Thus God made the firmament, and divided the waters which were under the firmament from the waters which were above the firmament; and it was so. And God called the firmament Heaven. So the evening and the morning were the second day. Then God said, "Let the waters under the heavens be gathered together into one place, and let the dry land appear"; and it was so. And God called the dry land Earth, and the gathering together of the waters He called Seas. And God saw that it was good. Then God said, "Let the earth bring forth grass, the herb that yields seed, and the fruit tree that yields fruit according to its kind, whose seed is in itself, on the earth"; and it was so. And the earth brought forth grass, the herb that yields seed according to its kind, and the tree that yields fruit, whose seed is in itself according to its kind. And God saw that it was good. So the evening and the morning were the third day. Then God said, "Let there be lights in the firmament of the heavens to divide the day from the night; and let them be for signs and seasons, and for days and years; and let them be for lights in the firmament of the heavens to give light on the earth"; and it was so. Then God made two great lights: the greater light to rule the day, and the lesser light to rule the night. He made the stars also. God set them in the firmament of the heavens to give light on the earth, and to rule over the day and over the night, and to divide the light from the darkness. And God saw that it was good. So the evening and the morning were the fourth day. Then God said, "Let the waters abound with an abundance of living creatures, and let birds fly above the earth across the face of the firmament of the heavens." So God created

great sea creatures and every living thing that moves, with which the waters abounded, according to their kind, and every winged bird according to its kind. And God saw that it was good. And God blessed them, saying, "Be fruitful and multiply, and fill the waters in the seas, and let birds multiply on the earth." So the evening and the morning were the fifth day. Then God said, "Let the earth bring forth the living creature according to its kind: cattle and creeping thing and beast of the earth, each according to its kind"; and it was so. And God made the beast of the earth according to its kind, cattle according to its kind, and everything that creeps on the earth according to its kind. And God saw that it was good. Then God said, "Let Us make man in Our image, according to Our likeness; let them have dominion over the fish of the sea, over the birds of the air, and over the cattle, over al the earth and over every creeping thing that creeps on the earth." So God created man in His own image; in the image of God He created him; male and female He created them. Then God blessed them, and God said to them, "Be fruitful and multiply; fill the earth and subdue it; have dominion over the fish of the sea, over the birds of the air, and over every living thing that moves on the earth." And God said, "See, I have given you every herb that yields seed which is on the face of all the earth, and every tree whose fruit yields seed; to you it shall be for food. Also, to every beast of the earth, to every bird of the air, and to everything that creeps on the earth, in which there is life, I have given every green herb for food"; and it was so. Then God saw everything that He had made, and indeed it was very good. So the evening and the morning were the sixth day. Thus the heavens and the earth, and all the host of them, were finished. And on the seventh day God ended His work which He had done, and He rested on the seventh day from all His work which He had done. Then God blessed the seventh day and sanctified it, because in it He rested from all His work which God had created and made. This is the history of the heavens and the earth when they were created, in the day that the Lord God made the earth and the heavens, before any plant of the field was in the earth and before any herb of the field had grown. For the Lord God had not caused it to rain on the earth, and there was no man to till the ground; but a mist went up from the earth and watered the whole face of the ground. And the Lord God formed man of the dust of the ground, and breathed into his nostrils the breath of life; and man became a living being. (Genesis 1:1–27)

Sorry, that was a long scripture and a lot to absorb, so you may want to think about it for a minute before continuing.

Do you think all of that came out of the big bang theory, or your cousin Clyde, the ape at your local zoo? We hope you can agree that God is the author of heaven and earth as well as the author of your faith. If you never read the Bible before, you will see the progression of this Creator as you read through it. It does not just stop at this one scripture; it goes on and on and on. Never ending and always revealing. How can one say they do not believe in God after they get to meet him and learn his ways by reading the Bible?

Here is where we may lose some of you that have a hard time with religion or creation. We know that not everyone who reads this guidebook will already be a Christian or even believes in creation. Maybe you do not want to believe in God. Please reconsider chapter three, not because we are telling you or trying to be persuasive in anyway, but because we love you and want you to step out of the darkness and into the light. Also, we want you to walk in freedom and not be bound by the addiction any longer than necessary. We are not trying to force any religion on anyone, but we are telling you the truth about the one who can help you stop your pain.

You see, here at AFL, we believe that God, Jesus, and Holy Spirit are the only way. If it were not so, all the other programs would be filled with people walking in freedom instead of a bondage that says they will always be an addict.

Now that we have revealed your Heavenly Father to you, we hope you will allow him in your heart to join with you in this battle for freedom. Please proceed to the next step and allow him to walk right beside you as he holds your hand through life's journey.

How do you see yourself?

On the road to freedom!

Step 3

I have decided to confess salvation according to Romans 10:9–10.

> *That if you confess with your mouth the Lord Jesus and believe in your heart that God has raised him from the dead, you will be saved. For with the heart one believes unto righteousness, and with the mouth confession is made unto salvation.*

Now before we give you the opportunity to make this confession, in what is called the salvation prayer, let us start with a short teaching on salvation and what it means so you know what and why you are asking God into your heart.

In the *Webster's Dictionary of the English Language,*[1] the meaning of salvation is

1. the act of saving from harm or loss.
2. the state of being thus saved.
3. a means of being thus saved.
4. deliverance from the power and penalty of sin.

Let us use excerpts from a chapter in *An Injection of Faith: One Addict's Journey to Deliverance*[2] to help bring you to your destiny. The title of the chapter was "Come and Go with Me." You might be saying, "Go where with you? Why do you want me to join you? Why must one be born again? What does it mean to be baptized and how or when should I?" Of course we are talking about going to heaven, and we want you to go with us because God loves you and does not want to see you go to hell, and neither do we! The scriptures say that Jesus told these words to Nicodemus, a ruler among the Jews:

Jesus answered him, I assure you, most solemnly I tell you, that unless a person is born again (anew, from above), he cannot ever see (know, be acquainted with, and experience) the kingdom of God. Nicodemus said to Him, How can a man be born when he is old? Can he enter his mother's womb again and be born? Jesus answered, I assure you, most solemnly I tell you, unless a man is born of water and [even] the Spirit, he cannot (ever) enter the kingdom of God. What is born of [from] the flesh is flesh [of the physical is physical]; and what is born of the Spirit is spirit. Marvel not [do not be surprised, astonished] at my telling you, you must all be born anew (from above). (John 3:3–7, AMP).

Can you see how important it is for one to enter salvation? He calls it being born anew, which is another way of saying you are allowing the Holy Spirit, who is the third person of the Trinity, to join with your spirit. Your old ways are no longer counted against you, and God receives you into himself. If you never had a father protect you from harm, this will be a little harder to understand. God is always for you, and when you ask him into your life, he spiritually has the right to be your Father. He will never leave you or forsake you. He will go to battle for you when someone comes against you. He will be your provider in times of need. He will walk beside you when you are lonely. God is everything you need, nothing lacking. Salvation is God's way of providing his people deliverance from sin and a spiritual death through repentance and faith in Jesus Christ. Salvation starts with repentance, which means that you are sorry for something you did in the past by either an action or an attitude about something.

Let us back up a little. Are you aware that when Adam and Eve ate the apple from the tree of life, they rebelled against God, and sin entered the world? They were separated from God because of that sin, and the wages of sin is death. Our death is not enough to cover the payment, and that is where the most famous scripture in the world applies, John 3:16: *"For God so greatly loved and dearly prized the world that He [even] gave up His only begotten (unique) Son, so that whoever believes in (trusts in, clings to, relies on) Him shall not perish (come to destruction, be lost) but have eternal (everlasting) life"* (AMP).

So because God gave Jesus, then it must be a gift to all that believe in him. It is God's grace on mankind because the wages of sin is death. In Revelation, the last book of the Bible, it is the account of the Apostle John being caught up into heaven through a vision, and in one of his encounters: there he was, face-to-face with an angel (a messenger of God) who told him not to put a seal on the book of prophecies (which really is the whole Bible, not just Revelations). The reason is at the return of Jesus, he will bring his wages and rewards to repay and render to each one just what his own actions and his own work deserves. You can read about this in Revelation 22 starting in verse 10 to about verse 16. And in verse 17, it reads like this: *"The [Holy] Spirit and the bride (the church, the true Christians) say, Come! And let him who is listening say, Come! And let everyone come who is thirsty [who is painfully conscious of his need of those things by which the soul is refreshed, supported, and strengthened]; and whoever [earnestly] desires to do it, let him come, take, appropriate, and drink the water of Life without cost"* (AMP).

Are you listening? Is your soul crying out because it is thirsty? You do not know how to quench that thirst, which is why you rely on the addiction, hoping that it will go away. But it does not; the only water that can do it is the water of life— Jesus himself. What are your wages and rewards going to be? The wages found in Romans 6:23? Will the rewards be the first half of verse 11 of Revelation or will they be the second half of this verse? *"For the wages of sin is death, but the free gift of God is eternal life through Christ Jesus our Lord"* (Romans 6:23).

A couple of paragraphs back, we mentioned about grace on mankind. *Grace*, which means "kindness or unmerited favor," is the root of salvation, getting what you do not deserve. Have you ever had someone forgive you for something you did wrong to them? That was grace extended to you in the form of forgiveness. Has your vehicle ever broken down and left you stranded on the side of the road and someone left their nice warm bed to come and get you? That was grace extended to you in the form of kindness. By grace, we are saved and made right with God because when we confess our sin, God forgives.

You must understand that grace is the foundation to being a Christian. It is the innermost part of your faith and relationship with God. Grace is the vehicle by which God brings himself to you and restores you. It is God giving you what you need, not what you deserve. You deserve to be punished for your sins, but God offers you forgiveness because of his grace. That forgiveness is why you are able to experience blessings upon blessings. Just like the faith we talked about in chapter 3, grace is a gift that you accept in faith, and it only comes through Christ. It is the power of grace that will transform your life.

Here are a few scriptures on grace:

The Lord is gracious and compassionate, slow to anger and great in love. (Psalm 145:8)

Yet the Lord longs to be gracious to you; therefore he will rise up to show you compassion. For the Lord is a

God of justice. Blessed are all who wait for him! (Isaiah 30:18, NIV)

The law was given through Moses, but grace and truth came through Jesus Christ. (John 1:17)

I do not treat the grace of God as meaningless. For if keeping the law could make us right with God, then there was no need for Christ to die. (Galatians 2:21)

Another part of salvation is mercy, which is not getting what you deserve or withholding punishment.

But God, who is rich in mercy, because of His great love with which He loved us, even when we were dead in trespasses, made us alive together with Christ (by grace you have been saved), and raised us up together, and made us sit together in the heavenly places in Christ Jesus, that in the ages to come He might show the exceeding riches of His grace in His kindness toward us in Christ Jesus. For by grace you have been saved through faith, and that not of yourselves; it is the gift of God, not of works, lest anyone should boast. (Ephesians 2:4–9)

Think about this…the addiction you are bound to might be something that could have killed you. Maybe you miraculously avoided an accident you should have been in due to reckless or even drunk driving. You are eating all the wrong foods that should have exploded your heart. You got yourself into so much debt because of gambling, you were not able to pay back the loans, so instead of being put into jail, they let you make small payments. There are angels sent by God that are working on your behalf administering his mercy.

How about all the times you are not aware of when God was there with his mercy. So, do you think that this may be possible? Let us put it this way: if you are reading this and you have an addiction, then yes, it is possible. We like to say it this way: for such a time as this that God is giving you a chance to know that he is real, and you have a chance to live again.

Now regarding the location of the sinner's prayer in the Bible? Well, there is not one mentioned; it is only implied. The basis of the sinner's prayer comes from Romans 10:9–10

"That if you confess with your mouth the Lord Jesus and believe in your heart that God has raised Him from the dead, you will be saved. For with the heart one believes unto righteousness, and with the mouth confession is made unto salvation."

Please note: the salvation prayer below is not any official prayer but rather a sample prayer to follow when asking Jesus into your heart. You can pray to God in your own words. Are you ready? Are you ready to lay your life down for the work of the cross? We hope you said yes because it is time for you to join us at the Lamb's dinner table that is prepared for you.

Read this prayer out loud. If you have to stop and go find a place to do it, please do, you will not regret it.

Dear, God in heaven, I come to you in the name of Jesus. I acknowledge to you and myself that I am a sinner, and I am sorry for my sins and the life that I have lived. I need your forgiveness to be in my life. Father, I know I cannot get rid of this addiction alone. Only you and you alone can take it from me and deliver me. I surrender my will over to you and ask that you make me clean as snow, like you did with so many others. Give me the same power they have seen so I too can see clearly. I believe that your only begotten Son, Jesus Christ, shed his precious blood on the cross at Calvary and died for my sins, and I am now willing to turn from my sin. You said in, Romans 10:9, that if we confess the Lord our God and believe in our hearts that God raised Jesus from the dead, we shall be saved. Right now, I confess Jesus as the Lord of my soul. With my heart, I believe that God raised Jesus from the dead. I accept Jesus Christ as my own personal savior, and according to your word, right now, I am saved. I thank you God, for your unlimited grace given to me by Jesus. I thank you that your grace always leads to repentance. Therefore I ask that, through the work of Jesus, you transform my life right now so that I may bring glory and honor to you alone and not to myself. I thank you for giving me eternal life. I thank you for your mercy, even when I was not aware of it. I ask and give permission to the Holy Spirit to lead the way. Amen!

If you just said this prayer and you meant it with all your heart, we believe that you just got saved and are born again. All of heaven is rejoicing, friend, so rejoice because you will be sitting with us at the Lamb's dinner table when he returns for us. Please let us know by visiting the website; we would love to add you to a list of names that we pray over.

You may ask, "Now that I am saved, what's next?" Time to be baptized. First, you can go through the rest of the steps knowing that as it is written in Romans 8:28–29 (AMP): *"We are assured and know that [God being a partner in their labor] all things work together and are [fitting into a plan] for good to and for those who love God and are called according to [His] design and purpose. For those whom He foreknew [of whom He was aware and loved beforehand], He also destined from the beginning [foreordaining them] to be molded into the image of His Son [and share inwardly His likeness], that He might become the firstborn among many brethren."*

In this part of the book of Romans, which was written by the Apostle Paul, Paul's gratitude, purpose, and mission emerge in this epistle. Convinced that all men are lost without Christ, Paul is thankful that there has been imparted to him this righteousness of God. He is not ashamed of the gospel but is determined to make Christ known to men everywhere. You should follow his lead because when you put God first, all other things will fall into place.

After digesting what we just mentioned, you need to get into a Bible-based church and study God's Word. Once you have found a church home, you will want to be baptized in water. By accepting Christ, you are baptized in the Spirit, but it is through water baptism that you show your obedience to the Lord. Water baptism is a symbol of your salvation from the dead. You were dead, but now you live, for the Lord Jesus Christ has redeemed you for a price! The price was his death on the cross. If you are born once, you will die twice, but who is born twice will die once!

We want to add a little something for those of you who may be saying you are already baptized, maybe as a baby. Being baptized is not when you are a baby; one must be aware of this decision to fulfill the truth of the scriptures. We have searched the scriptures and have not found anything that tells us to baptize our babies. We have found where it tells us to dedicate them: 1 Samuel 1:11, 26–28 (i.e., Jehovah is Jesus). A baby dedication is a ceremony where parents make a commitment before the Lord that they will train that child up in the ways of the Lord (Proverbs 22:6). So to finish the answer to the question found in the beginning of this step, one should be baptized after they receive the free gift of salvation and not before. If you were baptized as an adult before, and you are rededicating your life back to the Lord; it is fine to be baptized again. Actually, scripture does not mention anything about the limited times of being baptized. Any spiritual leader has the authority to baptize you, and it can even be done in your bathtub or swimming pool.

One of the first things you need to start off with is forgiveness. You will need to start with forgiving yourself and then anyone who has hurt you. This frees you up for the Holy Spirit to fill you with the love of God.

Remember, addiction is a stronghold, and only through the help of Jesus Christ can you overcome it and put it under your feet. You have to be saved in order for you to have authority to overcome addictive behavior. Stay in the word, grow in the Spirit, and know you are loved.

How do you see yourself?

On the road to freedom!

Step 4

I have made a list of all my sins

What is the definition of sin? *Sin* is anything that is contrary to the law or will of God. In her book, *Sin and the Church*, Crystal Maria Scott, says sin is "transgression of theological principles; an act, thought, or way of behaving that goes against the law or teachings of a religion, especially when the person who commits it is aware of this shameful offense; something that offends a moral or ethical principle; estrangement from God. In Christian theology, the condition of being denied God's grace because of a sin or sins committed. Knowingly do wrong, to commit a sin, especially by knowingly violating the law or teachings of a religion."[1]

It is a small word with a huge impact on one's outcome. It is a form of disobedience or rebellion against God. Sin is sinning no matter what way you look at it, and the Bible says that the wages of sin is death.

> *For the wages of sin is death, but the free gift of God is eternal life in Christ Jesus our Lord.* (Romans 6:23)

The truth is, we all sin. The Bible makes this apparent in scriptures such as Romans 3:23, *"For all have sinned and fall short of the glory of God"* (NIV), and 1 John 1:10 (ASV), *"If we say that we have not sinned, we make him a liar, and his word is not in us."* The Bible also says that God hates sin and encourages us as Christians to stop sinning: *"Those who have been born into God's family do not make a practice of sinning, because God's life is in them"* (1 John 3:9, NLT). Further complicating the matter are Bible passages that seem to suggest that some sins are debatable, and that sin is not always "black and white." What is sin for one Christian, for example, may not be sin for another Christian. So in light of all of these considerations, what attitude should we have toward sin? If you know it is wrong, do not do it!

Do not feel that you have to do this in one night or at one sitting; it will be done in stages—in most cases, a lifetime. You will work this step along with step 5 basically at the same time. You will start off with the ones you know off the top of your head by writing them down and then do step 5, and then when you are done with the known ones, you will seek guidance through prayer and meditation for God to reveal any hidden sins. As he shows them to you, you will write them down and then repent for them. This is a form of deliverance a.k.a., inventory.

This is going to be hard for most people because it is hard to accept ourselves, and that is why we got into an addiction in the first place. However, the more you do it, the easier it will become. Once you start to peel off the layers of guilt, shame, self-pity, hopelessness, failure, and depression, the frustration, anger, and fear will start to fade away. The key is to get honest with yourself; if you think it, it must be true. The purpose of this step is not to get you to see how horrible you are but to release you from the bondage sin has placed in your life. Do not beat yourself up when it comes to memory; just turn it over to God and lay it at the foot of the cross. Remember, it is the work of the cross that puts sin under his feet. This is meant to be a relief valve, not a judgment session.

You may be asking yourself, "How honest do I have to be?" The answer to that question is found on the basis of "How free do you want to be?" The deeper you go into the depth of your sin, the clearer you will see the future. This list is not meant to be shared with anyone else unless you want to. This list is between you and God, who is the author of forgiveness. No man needs to see it so you can be forgiven. You can get as nasty as your past or as honest as a child. The list will fit your lifestyle.

Here is something we found out about taking a list of our sins. Feelings were triggered that overwhelmed our pain and caused us to panic, thinking that if we allow those feelings back into our lives, we will use again. What we also found out is if we avoid our old feelings, that cause us to get into an addiction in the first place, the tension becomes too much for us, and we were not honest with ourselves. Fear of the unknown can override our fear of failure. Do not operate in fear but in love for yourself.

This is the time and place to get free! No holding back! Remember, this is not just a one-time action. You could be adding to your list for years to come. It depends on how much junk you have. The workbook has a section for you to write down your list.

How do you see yourself?

On the road to freedom!

Step 5

I have repented with my mouth and asked forgiveness for each one of those sins.

> *If we confess our sins, he is faithful and just and will forgive us our sins and purify us from all unrighteousness.* (1 John 1:9, NIV)

We hope you are being very honest with your list in the last step. Because if you keep sin a secret, the devil will use it against you; but when you expose it and confess it out loud, it is now covered under the word. When you are being truthful, God's truth will overshadow you and help you see, hear, and know differently. Repenting is a big part of your new life. It may be the first time you ever got honest with yourself.

What does it mean to repent? When you repent, you should feel remorse for the sin in such a way that you change from your old ways of thinking and doing. What does that mean in layman's terms? Changing your mind! If you truly accept Christ into your heart, your old person will die spiritually, along with the addiction, and you will never want to do those things you did any longer.

If you are willing to let your past actions go, then this step is going to be easy to do. When we say to repent and change your mind, we are not saying to just have a different thought. You have to be willing to do things differently. Think differently. Act differently. Treat people differently. Everything about you has to be altered into a new way.

That is why it is important for you to confess your sins out loud. In most cases, if you hear it and it does not sound right, your conscience will want to do something about it. We want you to now take the list from step 4 and go line by line, confessing each sin you have written down using the prayer below. After you have gone through the list, you will use this prayer for each one you remember hours, days, weeks, months, and even years to come.

> *Father God, according to 1 John 1:9, I confess (speak out the sin here) and ask you for your forgiveness to purify my soul and cleanse me from unrighteousness. I am sorry God, that I allowed this filth to rule and reign over my life. I declare with my mouth that (speak out the sin here) will no longer have possession over my life. I take this sin and lay it at the foot of the cross where Jesus now has control over it. I thank you Father, for the Holy Spirit, who lives inside me, to help me overcome this area. Amen!*

Now was that so bad? How does it feel to do something right? Now take what you just did by faith and believe that each sin has been erased from your name and give a shout of joy unto the Lord! Keep up the good work!

After going through your list of muddy waters in step 4, you may have missed one sin that most people are not aware of: forgiving others. Unforgiveness is a sin and plays a big part with repentance. Even the best relationships can have unforgiveness in them. Since forgiveness goes against our nature, you must forgive by faith, whether you feel like it or not. You must trust God to do the work in you that needs to be done so that the forgiveness will be complete. "And I am convinced and sure of this very thing, that He Who began a good work in you will continue until the day of Jesus Christ [right up to the time of His return], developing [that good work] and perfecting and bringing it to full completion in you" (Philippians 1:6, AMP).

Part of the forgiveness process is not just asking God to forgive you but for you to forgive others. Sometimes, when we ask God to forgive us for something we did, he will tell us to first forgive our brother. In Luke 6:37 (NIV), he says, "Forgive, and you will be forgiven." Also scripture says, "For if you forgive other people when they sin against you, your heavenly Father will also forgive you. But, if you do not forgive others their sins, your Father will not forgive your sins" (Matthew 6:14–15, NIV).

Forgiveness releases a person from criticism and also releases them from being imprisoned by their own negative judgments. It has been proven in some studies that when a person has unforgiveness, he or she is actually murdering themselves. A great teaching on unforgiveness is Jesus's parable of the unmerciful servant, recorded in Matthew 18:21–35. In the parable, the king forgives an exceptionally large debt, which in reality could never be repaid, of one of his servants. Later on, that same servant refuses to forgive the small debt of another man. The king hears about this and rescinds his prior forgiveness. Jesus finishes the parable by saying, *"This is how my heavenly father will treat each of you unless you forgive your brother from your heart."*

Do not be confused here; God's forgiveness is not based on our works but only by our faith in the work of the cross.

Not that any one step is more important than another, but this one is remarkably close to being set apart. If you took step 1 by knowing that you have a problem and you admitted it, then you accepted God for who he really is and took him into your heart. If you went to step 4 and made a list of your sins and repented for them, even went right to finishing the other steps by asking people to forgive you and decided to pray every day and pick up your cross on a daily basis by walking with God, you will never complete the links of the chain that are needed to bind this addiction. This is what could happen when you have unforgiveness against someone and even yourself.

Forgiveness might be harder to do than taking that first step, but it is worth it because it is good for your health. Unforgiveness can be more dangerous than cancer. It spreads and can create changes in your body. Carrying a grudge, bitterness, or carrying anger can cause a lot of damage to your body, especially if you have worn down your body already. This can lead to high blood pressure, heart disease, emotional stress, brain damage—and it can even affect the body's immune system. This is only a small list of what can happen to your body when you do not let the unforgiveness go. We suggest if you want to learn more about how this can affect your body, research unforgiveness.

You might be justifying why you cannot forgive someone right now. The bottom line is, whatever you are thinking outside of forgiveness is not the truth. It is part of the sin nature to hate, coupled with not being able to release whatever a person did to you. We believe God honors our commitment to obey him and our desire to please him when we choose to forgive. He completes the work in his time. You must continue to forgive by faith, until the work of forgiveness is done in your heart. You have to be willing to go through this process in order for faith to take root.

Through the sacrifice that Christ did on the cross to forgive us, we must do the same thing in forgiving others. His work was as if we never sinned, giving us a clean slate. Hebrews 10:17 says, *"Their sins and lawless acts I will remember no more."* Forgetting is a bit harder than forgiveness, yet you cannot truly forgive someone without giving them a fresh start. That is what you have when Christ is your Lord, a fresh start.

As it was so eloquently stated by Henry Ward Beecher, "I can forgive, but I cannot forget, is only another way of saying, I will not forgive. Forgiveness ought to be like a canceled note—torn in two, and burned up, so that it never can be shown against one."[1]

Forgiveness is a choice! Say it out loud: "I choose to forgive myself for (speak out the offense). I choose to forgive (speak out the name) for doing (speak out the act), and I choose to forget it as well.

Forgiveness does not change the past, but it enhances the future!

How do you see yourself?

On the road to freedom!

Step 6

I have asked God for forgiveness and to remove any guilt or shame I put on myself.

> *And whatever you ask in My name, that I will do, that the Father may be glorified in the Son. If you ask anything in My name, I will do it.* (John 14:13–14)

In the last step we talked about unforgiveness and how to forgive others. This step is to help you forgive yourself so God can fill you up with good things. It is the peace of God that will remove any memory, so if you replace the guilt or shame with heaven-sent peace, you can have authority over this area. In John 14:27, Jesus was sitting around the table talking to his disciples, and he said these words, *"Peace I leave with you, My peace I give to you; not as the world gives do I give to you. Let not your heart be troubled, neither let it be afraid."* Let peace be your umpire in everything you do. If Holy Spirit is not giving you peace, do not force anything just because you want it. Learn to let the fruit of self-control be exercised as the character of Jesus is being developed inside you. It is going to take discipline, but you are guaranteed to mature, grow, and begin to enjoy life in the spirit of the living God...a wonderful reward.

Forgiveness does not change what has happened in your past, but it puts a whole new meaning to your destiny. It is designed to allow you to walk forward into your future. If you live in your past, you can never reach what God has placed in your future. Living in your past is like being institutionalized; every day you are reminded of the crime that put you in there. The good news about God is you have been pardoned for your sins. Those of you that have been in jail or prison know how important it is to be pardoned for your crime. Some of you might still be institutionalized right now and would love to be pardoned. You need to step out from the sin into a life of freedom. Just like so many people have given of their life for freedom in the United States of America, Jesus has given his life for your freedom of sin by putting your sin upon himself, which means you no longer need to carry it.

Forgiveness is a choice you make through a decision of your will, motivated by obedience to God and his command to forgive. In the *Merriam-Webster's Collegiate Dictionary,*[1] one of the meanings of guilt is "a bad feeling caused by knowing or thinking that you have done something bad or wrong...and for shame they have: a feeling of guilt, regret, or sadness that you have because you know you have done something wrong., ability to feel guilt, regret, or embarrassment., dishonor or disgrace..."

Shame can be explained as the discomfort people feel when they do not live up to the expectations of others or the remorse and/or embarrassment they feel when they think they have let others down. Guilt and its partner, shame, can paralyze one's mind.

Guilt and shame are emotions and can come in many different forms and will hit just about every single person at some time in their life. The effects of them are based on how one can deal or cope with life. Like other emotions, there is not one explanation. Guilt and shame can be put in one's mind by something they feel they did wrong or by what others may have said. The traditional view is they reside under the surface veneer of our behavior. The psychodynamic theory proposes that we build defense mechanisms to protect us from the guilt and shame we would experience if we knew just how awful our awful desires really were.[2]

Guilt and shame can be devastating not only to one's mind but to their body as well. It can take a perfect body and change the physical appearance to make it look like it is much older, as well as affect the health. It is important to understand the differences between them. Shame can be the stronger of the two.

Here is a quote from Beverly Engel, a psychotherapist for more than thirty years: "In his book, *Shame: The Power of Caring*, clinical psychologist Gershen Kaufman explains that the meaning of the two experiences is as different as feeling inadequate is from feeling immoral." Engel continues to say, "In this comparison, immoral goes with guilt and inadequate goes with shame."

Engel adds "that another clear distinction I've heard is that guilt is when you feel disappointed in yourself for violating your own personal value system or your own code of behavior while shame is when you actually feel disappointed in yourself because you failed in your own mind in some way, whether you failed to cope with something or a failure or weakness of yours has been exposed in front of other people who define it as wrong."

Still, Engel says, "Another way to distinguish the two is to think of it this way: when we feel guilt, we feel badly about something we did or neglected to do and our conscious bothers us whereas when we feel shame, we feel badly about who we are in general. Shame is the most destructive of human emotions. Shame destroys a person's self-esteem and sense of who they are and causes people really serious problems. It's the core issue of addiction and can cause other issues like suicide, depression and anger,"[3] If you would like to read more articles from her, visit her website at www.beverlyengel.com.

Let us put it this way, guilt is seeing what you have done, shame is seeing yourself as a failure because of what you have done. God sees you as a great Picasso, no matter what you have done. That deserves a big hallelujah shout!

The good news is that no matter how serious the sin, God is always seeking us out and is willing to forgive and forget our sins and give us a fresh start. As long as we live, it is never too late to ask for forgiveness and make a new start! God wants to forgive, and it starts when we ask him. He is not looking down on you debating whether you deserve it or if he should extend his grace. He loves you so much that he will extend his grace first and then forgive all that you have done at the same time. Remember, asking God for forgiveness is a choice, and the main requirement is for you to repent. *Repentance* means a sincere resolve to turn away from sin and toward God! First John 1:9 says that if we repent and confess our sins, God is faithful to forgive us.

You do not need to walk around carrying a load of guilt. The Apostle Paul says, *"Since all have sinned and are falling short of the honor and glory which God bestows and receives. [All] are justified and made upright and in right standing with God, freely and gratuitously by His grace (His unmerited favor and mercy), through the redemption which is [provided] in Christ Jesus"* (Romans 3:23–24, AMP).

You need to get it deep down inside how much God loves you and forgives you. The deeper it goes, the freer you will become. Never- ending forgiveness, it goes on and on and on until the day you meet him face-to -face. He wants you to *"keep vigilant watch over your heart; that's where life starts. Do not talk out of both sides of your mouth; avoid careless banter, white lies, and gossip. Keep your eyes straight ahead; ignore all sideshow distractions. Watch your step, and the road will stretch out smooth before you. Look neither right nor left; leave evil in the dust"* (Proverbs 4:25, MSG).

Are you ready to enhance your future? Let us get started! Here is a short prayer to pray:

Lord, please forgive me for what I have done to you and myself. I offer up this forgiveness prayer in hopes that you will look at my mistakes no more. I know that what I did was wrong and against your word, but I hope that you will forgive me just as you forgave others like me.

I will try Lord, to change. I will make every attempt to not give in to temptation again. I know that you are the most important thing in my life right now. I ask for your guidance to help me overcome the shame and guilt I placed on myself and for allowing others to dictate my future. I forgive myself for all of my wrongs. I know that I am not a bad person and will go easy on myself. Bless me Lord. Amen!

How do you see yourself?
On the road to freedom!

Step 7

I have been delivered from all unrighteousness.

> *Delight yourself in the Lord, and he will give you the desire of your heart. Commit your ways to the Lord, trust in him, and he will act. He will bring forth your righteousness as the light, and your justice as the noonday.* (Psalm 37:4–6, ESV)

Unrighteousness is the noun from the root word unrighteous. *Webster's New World Dictionary[1]* meaning is

1. not righteous; wicked; sinful.
2. Not right; unjust; unfair.

In other words, it can be said that it is a person performing a sinful or wicked act or something evil. We can even go as far as to say it can be someone who does not love God or the things of God. In Romans 1:18–32, God's wrath on unrighteousness is said like this:

> *For the wrath of God is revealed from heaven against all ungodliness and unrighteousness of men, who suppress the truth in unrighteousness, because what may be known of God is manifest in them, for God has shown it to them. For since the creation of the world His invisible attributes are clearly seen, being understood by the things that are made, even His eternal power and Godhead, so that they are without excuse, because, although they knew God, they did not glorify Him as God, nor were thankful, but became futile in their thoughts, and their foolish hearts were darkened. Professing to be wise, they became fools, and changed the glory of the incorruptible God into an image made*

like corruptible man—and birds and four-footed animals and creeping things. Therefore God also gave them up to uncleanness, in the lusts of their hearts, to dishonor their bodies among themselves, who exchanged the truth of God for the lie, and worshiped and served the creature rather than the Creator, who is blessed forever. Amen. For this reason God gave them up to vile passions. For even their women exchanged the natural use for what is against nature. Likewise also the men, leaving the natural use of the woman, burned in their lust for one another, men with men committing what is shameful, and receiving in themselves the penalty of their error which was due. And even as they did not like to retain God in their knowledge, God gave them over to a debased mind, to do those things which are not fitting; being filled with all unrighteousness, sexual immorality, wickedness, covetousness, maliciousness; full of envy, murder, strife, deceit, evil-mindedness; they are whisperers, backbiters, haters of God, violent, proud, boasters, inventors of evil things, disobedient to parents, undiscerning, untrustworthy, unloving, unforgiving, unmerciful; who, knowing the righteous judgment of God, that those who practice such things are deserving of death, not only do the same but also approve of those who practice them.

Wow, you can see that if we stop here, we are all doomed according to God's word. But God loves us too much to just stop here. He has made a way for us to be delivered from all unrighteousness. So this is a good place for 1 John 1:9: *"If we confess our sins, he is faithful and just to forgive us our sins, and to cleanse us from all unrighteousness."*

If you have made your list in step 4 and confessed them in step 5, asked God for forgiveness in step 7, you have been cleansed from unrighteousness. Rejoice!

How do you see yourself?

On the road to freedom!

Step 8

I have asked God to show me all persons I have hurt and made a list.

> *And be kind to one another, tenderhearted, forgiving one another, even as God in Christ forgave you.* (Ephesians 4:32)

Just like in step 4 where you made a list of your sins, you are going to use this step to make a list of all the people you have hurt from as far back as you can remember. Again, this list will continue to grow as time goes by. You will be amazed that four, five, or even twenty years from now, you will remember someone and run to this list to write down their name. Next to each name you might want to put how you felt at the time.

A lot of times, depending on the addiction, a person may not even know that they hurt someone. If you have a problem with alcohol or drugs, you might have been in a blackout and do not remember a particular night. Sometimes with other addictions, we are so into ourselves that we make a move without thinking and do not realize that that move just hurt someone. It could have been a spoken word or maybe a gesture that made the other person mad. Sometimes it could be just for the fact that we were not around to help with the kids or housework.

A hurt can range from one word to driving drunk and killing someone. Either way, the hurt was taken in offense and became a stumbling block. This is a dual process and not only hurts them; it hurts you too. There are hundreds of scriptures that talk about the tongue or spoken word and about how our actions can cause someone to fall. Here are just a few:

Death and life are in the power of the tongue, and those who love it will eat its fruits. (Proverbs 18:21)

For Whoever desires to love life and see good days, let him keep his tongue from evil and his lips from speaking deceit. (1 Peter 3:10, ESV)

A soft answer turns away wrath, but a harsh word stirs up anger. (Proverbs 15:1)

And the tongue is a fire, a world of unrighteousness. The tongue is set among our members, staining the whole body, setting on fire the entire course of life, and set on fire by hell. (James 3:6, ESV)

But what comes out of the mouth proceeds from the heart, and this defiles a person. For out of the heart come evil thoughts, murder, adultery, sexual immorality, theft, false witness, slander. (Matthew 15:18–19, ESV)

Therefore let us not judge one another anymore, but rather resolve this, not to put a stumbling block or a cause to fall in our brother's way. (Romans 14:13)

You may ask why you have to make a list of all the people you have hurt. The answer to that question is found throughout the Bible, but one of the main reasons is one must forgive themselves before the person they hurt can forgive them. That is why we put steps 4, 5 and 6 first so you get to see yourself for what you once were. Now without all that guilt and shame clouding up your judgment, it will be easier for you to be honest. This may come as a little bit of a shock to you, but no matter how old you are, there are people in your past you have hurt. It is time to come out of your insecurities and denials and stop blaming others for your own mistakes.

Plus, it is part of your freedom to know that you have forgiven yourself for hurting another person. Writing a list typically does not mean you have to have forgiveness from them. Not everybody on your list will need to be approached, and some of the ones you do approach still will not forgive you, or they may forgive you but not trust you again. This is understandable and allowed, so do not think just because they do not trust you right off the bat, they are wrong, especially in a codependent setting. Sometimes a hurt relationship may be damaged beyond repair, but it is your willingness to ask for forgiveness that will heal your soul. God will help with this in the next step.

Here is a prayer that you can pray to help you get started with your list:

Father, I ask you for help with my hurt list. Help me to remember all the people I have hurt and the offense that caused that hurt. Help me to remember how I felt at that moment. Help me not to be afraid of bringing up these feelings but to know that you are near to love me and comfort me with the pain. I ask this in Jesus's name. Amen!

Now go get your workbook and start on your list. Take your time, but in the meanwhile, do not go back to the addiction.

How do you see yourself?

On the road to freedom!

Step 9

I have prayed over my hurt list seeking those I need to ask forgiveness from.

> *Therefore if you bring your gift to the altar, and there remember that your brother has something against you, leave your gift there before the altar, and go your way. First be reconciled to your brother, and then come and offer your gift.* (Matthew 5:23–24)

> *Confess your trespasses to one another, and pray for one another, that you may be healed. The effective, fervent prayer of a righteous man avails much.* (James 5:16)

In this step, you will pray about those you are to be reconciled with and make every attempt to ask them for their forgiveness in what you did to them. Broken relationships are not made right without someone seeking or offering forgiveness. Most people never make an attempt to mend a broken relationship because they refuse to take responsibility for what they did wrong. It is called pride! You will need to remove the pride from your heart and humble yourself to gain victory over this area. Forgiveness is not a mind game; it is one having a sincere change of the heart. In no way are you to approach a person in a manipulated way.

Asking for forgiveness when you know you should, is not a simple matter of uttering a few words. It is a way to show that you accept your mistake and have learned from it. Honesty is crucial; first, you must forgive yourself and then you must know that you are sorry for your actions so that when you approach the other person, they will be able to accept your apology a lot easier. This is why it is so important to first take it to prayer. God will help you if you ask.

When people forgive, it is as if the offense is being sent away. Scripture says that when God forgives, he no longer remembers. This works for both asking for forgiveness and forgiving others. When you forgive someone, yourself or someone forgiving you, it is sent away so it can no longer affect you, but those that have been hurt from your wrongs will need time to have trust restored. How much time, you may ask? As much time as necessary!

Common excuses for not asking for forgiveness is avoiding God's command to be reconciled with the other person. Sometimes when God asks us to do something, instead of obeying, we try to rationalize away the need to take action. With seeking forgiveness, our pride can get in the way, because asking for forgiveness requires us to humble ourselves before those we have offended.

Here are few of those thoughts we might tell ourselves:

- *It happened a long time ago.*

- *The one I wronged has moved away.*

- *It was such a small offense.*

- *Things have gotten better.*

- *I am just being too sensitive.*

- *No one's perfect.*

- *He/she will not understand.*

- *Making it right will involve money, where am I going to get that?*

- *I will do it later.*

- *I will only do it over again.*

- *The other person was mostly wrong.*

- *My parents will not understand when I tell them what I am doing.*

- *I will leave the worse offense until last.*

- *If I promise not to do it again, won't that be enough?*

- *They are not Christians—what will they think?*

- *If I go back, it will get my friend in trouble.*

In Matthew 5:23–24, Jesus commanded us to be reconciled with those we have offended. This is an amazing command! God wants us to be reconciled with those we have offended. If you have put off asking for forgiveness, do not delay any longer; go in humility, ask for forgiveness, and seek to be reconciled. Sometimes it might not be a good idea to approach someone, especially if you are the only one feeling the pain. This is why you have to write the list and pray over each name. God will tell you who not to go to. Please make sure this is from God and not because you are afraid.

You must think of how the offense occurred and then you should seek to relive the hurt through the eyes of the person that you offended. You should ask God for the ability to sense the feelings that he or she experienced. You must also determine whether or not you need to make any restitution as a consequence of the offense.

Before you approach the hurting person, you should be certain that you have identified the issues that offended him or her the most. When you repent for lesser offenses while failing to address the greater ones, you multiply the offense. It is important to make sure that the wordings you have planned for your apology implies no blame whatsoever to the other person. Your wording could be different if they are not a Christian. You may want to write out your apology and then practice saying it out loud. You need to clearly explain what you are sorry for without any excuses. Our workbook can help you with this exercise.

In no way are you to walk away with a disappointed feeling. If the person you are making restitution to does not want to forgive you, you need to turn around and shake the dust off as you walk away. In Matthew 10:14 (NIV), Jesus told the disciples, *"If anyone will not welcome you or listen to your words, leave that home or town and shake the dust off your feet."* In other words, do not take offense. You did your part, now it is time for God to do his part on them to help them sort out their feelings. They may not remember how much it hurt until you bring it back up. In time, they may come back to you and tell you they forgive you. Remember to be strong and show them that you have changed by your response. Do not go out screaming and yelling with profanity and gestures.

How do you see yourself?

On the road to freedom!

Step 10

I have denied myself and will pick up my cross daily.

> *Then he said to them all: "Whoever wants to be my disciple must deny themselves and take up their cross daily and follow me."* (Luke 9:23, NIV)

In that passage, Jesus is talking to the disciples after feeding the crowd of five thousand near a town called Bethsaida. He was telling them that he soon will be put to death and on the third day will rise again. It is a type and shadow of our spiritual death that we proclaim when we accept Jesus as our Lord. So to deny yourself means to say no to yourself and yes to God. It does not mean we must get crucified every day. Even Jesus got crucified only once. It means we should go about every day with the constant awareness of what Jesus had done at Calvary.

What does this mean? We are not talking about asceticism—forgoing earthly possessions, not eating certain foods, ignoring the world, things like that. We can say that the process of denial is to humbly submit your will to God. It is to go through life repeating the words that Jesus said the night before he died. When he was praying in the garden, he said to God his Father, *"Not my will but yours be done"* (Luke 22:42) It can also be found in the Lord's Prayer. *"Your will be done, on earth as it is in heaven"* (Matthew 6:10).

> *We like how Pope John Paul II said it, "When the cross is embraced it becomes a sign of love and of total self-giving. To carry it behind Christ means to be united with him in offering the greatest proof of love ...the choice is between a full life and an empty existence, between truth and falsehood."[1]*

What a beautiful way to put it. Since God is love, then doing the will of the Father is a sign of love. To carry your cross behind Jesus means he is in front of you showing you the path to take and the will of the Father. Our job is to walk behind him saying what he says and doing what he does. He is our advocate and will only speak what he hears the Father speak and will only do what he sees the Father do. For those of you who are parents, this may hit home for you. Can you recall, if they are there yet, when your child was little and everywhere you went, they were right behind you? They would repeat every word you said, even if you did not want them too. Maybe you are not a parent but can recall when you did that to your parents.

Well, that is exactly what we are talking about how we are to be. Your life is no longer yours but God's. He has your best interest at heart and will only show you the right paths to take and will only say the right words that need to be said at the right time. He says in John 10:27, *"My sheep hear my voice, and I know them, and they follow me."*

With that being said, to live as a follower of the Lord becomes the highest value, then all other values are given their rightful rank and importance. *"Do not lay up for yourselves treasures on earth, where moth and rust destroy and where thieves break in and steal; but lay up for yourselves treasures in heaven, where neither moth nor rust destroys and where thieves do not break in and steal. For where your treasure is, there your heart will be also"* (Matthew 6:19–21). Whoever depends solely on worldly goods will end up losing, even though there might seem to be an appearance of success. Death will find that person with an abundance of possessions but having lived a wasted life. Read Luke 12:13–21 for more of an in-depth understanding. Therefore the choice is between being and having, between a full life and an empty existence, between truth and falsehood. The idea is that nothing in this life is worth keeping if it means losing eternal life—not a job, not family, not a group of friends, not even your very identity. The call is tough, but the eternal reward is well worth the temporary pain. If you wonder if you are ready to take up your cross, consider these questions:

Are you willing to follow Jesus?

> ⇒ if it means losing some of your closest friends?

> ⇒ if it means alienation from your family?

> ⇒ if it means the loss of your reputation?

> ⇒ if it means losing your job?

> ⇒ if it means losing your life?

> ⇒ if it means losing the addictive ways?

Now, we are not saying that any of the first five will take place, but they could. We are in no means saying you have to leave your family and friends to follow Jesus, but in those rare occasions, one may have to. You do not disown; you walk away from being around them and then you continuously pray for them. If you disown them there is no hope for their return, but if you walk away there is hope that one day, they will understand why you did what you did and want to be part of your life. In most cases just living apart is good enough. You will have to be led by the Holy Spirit in what is best for you, not by your feelings.

We do know for sure that if you are willing to follow Jesus, the addictive behavior will be made easy. Easy in the sense that it will be easy to let go!

We are not saying that you have to give up health and wealth to pick up your cross. It just takes its rightful place when you put God first and submit to his will. We do not need to suffer even though it will be hard at times. Remember, you are looking toward him to get rid of the addictive behavior and to think differently about how to live differently.

Are you ready to surrender your will? This is not the time to walk alone. This is a time to believe in something greater than yourself who will walk beside you, guiding you as he speaks the proper steps to take and path to follow. Why would you not want to do something that someone has already done for you? Why would you want to do it alone? What in hell do you want? *Hell* is referencing to the place you do not want to be in. It was a place that you might be familiar with, but you do not want to live there.

Remember, you are not a sprint runner, you are in a marathon. Take deep breaths and exhale slowly while you aim for the mark so you can finish the race.

How do you see yourself?

On the road to freedom!

Step 11

I have made a conscious decision to trust God and live a life of prayer.

> *Trust in the Lord with all your heart, and lean not on your own understanding; In all of your ways acknowledge him, and he will direct your paths.* (Proverbs 3:5–6)

In this step, the prayer we are talking about is personal. This is not the time to pray for others; that type of prayer will come later. After we pick up our cross, we make the decision to lean on God. Through a life of prayer brings stability. Prayer is communicating not only our concerns but hearing what our Heavenly Father expects from us. This part of the prayer is when we sit quiet and meditate on his word.

Prayer is a bridge from our mess to God's rest! It is the conduit between the throne of God and earth that brings the power to us while keeping a message from being harmed by the outside elements.

In Ephesians chapter 6, it gives a parable on how we are to enter a life of prayer:

> *Finally, be strong in the Lord and in his mighty power. Put on the full armor of God, so that you can take your stand against the devil's schemes. For our struggle is not against flesh and blood, but against the rulers, against the authorities, against the powers of this dark world and against the spiritual forces of evil in the heavenly realms. Therefore put on the full armor of God, so that when the day of evil comes, you may be able to stand your ground, and after you have done everything, to stand. Stand firm then, with the belt of truth buckled around your waist, with the breastplate of righteousness in place, and with*

your feet fitted with the readiness that comes from the gospel of peace. In addition to all this, take up the shield of faith, with which you can extinguish all the flaming arrows of the evil one. Take the helmet of salvation and the sword of the Spirit, which is the word of God. And pray in the Spirit on all occasions with all kinds of prayers and requests. With this in mind, be alert and always keep on praying for all the Lord's people. Pray also for me, that whenever I speak, words may be given me so that I will fearlessly make known the mystery of the gospel, for which I am an ambassador in chains. Pray that I may declare it fearlessly, as I should. (Ephesians 6:10–20, NIV)

What does it mean to trust God? Trusting God simply means believing that he loves you, he is good all the time and he has the power to help you in every situation. You are relying on him! In John 15:5, Jesus says that apart from him, we can do nothing. He has to become your life source. You need to lean on him for help with everything in your life. God wants you to put him first in your life. He wants you to put your confidence and trust in him, all the time, in everything. That is why we used Proverbs 3:5–6 as our scripture for this step.

The best way to hear from God and know how he wants you to live is to know what the Bible says. God's word gives you wisdom and strength. As you study the Bible, your mind is renewed so you no longer just think the way the world thinks—you can think the way God thinks!

Do not be conformed to this world (this age), [fashioned after and adapted to its external, superficial customs], but be transformed (changed) by the [entire] renewal of your mind [by its new ideals and its new attitude], so that you may prove [for yourselves] what is the good and acceptable and perfect will of God, even the thing which

is good and acceptable and perfect [in His sight for you]
(Romans 12:2, AMP).

Here is another version:

And do not be conformed to this world, but be transformed by the renewing of your mind, that you may prove what is that good and acceptable and perfect will of God. (Romans 12:2)

Now, in order for you to trust God, you have to build up your faith. Faith is more than positive thinking. Positive thinking will not produce the faith you need to be an overcomer. The only way to develop faith is to learn to know God and that comes by hearing. Romans 10:17 says, *"So then faith comes by hearing, and hearing by the word of God."* Since he is trustworthy, as we learn to know him, we spontaneously learn to trust him. Faith is trusting God even when things do not turn out the way we expect.

But without faith it is impossible to please Him, for he who comes to God must believe that He is, and that He is a rewarder of those who diligently seek Him. (Hebrews 11:6)

You cannot create faith; you have to believe faith! You cannot work on being righteous any more than you can work on your faith. Both are gifts from God. They come as a result of knowing Jesus. Knowing Jesus comes as a result of spending time in prayer, fellowship, and having a relationship with him. If you reach out to him, he will give you the real faith that you need.

In 2 Corinthians 5:7, we are told to *"walk by faith and not by sight,"* so this is why this is a big step for you. It can be extremely hard to believe in something you cannot see or touch, and that is why AFL is so different than other twelve-step programs. Not that we want to say that other twelve-step programs are wrong, but they want to be politically correct. In other words, some of them say to pick the first thing that comes to your mind and trust in that until you can stand on your own— *"The God of your own understanding."*[1] Therefore if you do not believe in God, the program will still work for you. They are right: to a point. Anytime you take the focus and make a shift from one thought to another, the first thought will change. We call that renewing the mind. AFL teaches that there is freedom from addiction by the highest form of power—God! No other name is above him; therefore no other power has the power to heal you from the addiction. You have to turn your will over to him, not just make a decision.

That is an extremely dangerous place for someone who lost control of their life and now they are being told to pick something that is going to help them overcome. Our favorite one is using a chair. The chair becomes your god, and just because it holds you up, it does not mean it will not let you down.

Let us say one more thing on this: if that wood rots, do you think it will still hold you up? This is why AFL teaches you the truth. God will never let you down.

> *Be strong and of good courage, do not fear nor be afraid of them; for the Lord your God, He is the One who goes with you. He will not leave you nor forsake you.* (Deuteronomy 31:6)

The truth can only be found in his word, and that is why AFL believes that if you trust in God and live a life of prayer, you will overcome the addiction, and it will be put under your feet. In second Chronicles 7:14 it says, *"If my people who are called by My name will humble themselves, and pray and seek*

My face, and turn from their wicked ways, then I will hear from heaven, and will forgive their sin and heal their land." "Heal your land" can be a type and shadow of the addiction in your life. God is bigger than your circumstances and can handle anything you throw at him. There is nothing that you did that can come between you and him. That is why you will see a lot of scripture throughout this guidebook, because the word needs to become your higher power, not the chair. The word will build up your faith! What we say here at AFL will also be backed up by the word, so please do not think that you cannot follow this program because there is just too much of the word. Remember, it is the word that sets you free! We teach you to really know God, not just know about God. It is not about religion but about relationship!

Now that you are learning to trust God, it is time for you to learn how to pray. You may be asking, "How do I pray? I never did anything like this before." As you move and groove in your new way of life, you will change your prayer style, but one thing that should never change is entering into his courts with thanksgiving. Psalms 100:4 says, *"Enter into His gates with thanksgiving, And into His courts with praise. Be thankful to Him, and bless His name."* So be thankful that you have a chance to change your life. In the Bible, the disciples asked Jesus the same question, *"Lord, teach us to pray."* Jesus answered them with what is known as the Lord's Prayer, which actually is our prayer given to us by the Lord.

This is something that you should pray on a daily basis. It will help you to grow both spiritually and naturally. If you been around other 12-step programs you know that most all of them will start out meeting with this prayer.

Our Father in heaven,
Hallowed be Your name.
Your kingdom come.
Your will be done On earth as it is in heaven.
Give us this day our daily bread.
And forgive us our debts, As we forgive our debtors.
And do not lead us into temptation, But deliver us from
the evil one.
For Yours is the kingdom and the power and the glory
forever. Amen!
(Matthew 6:9–13)

PRAY: Praise, Repent, Acknowledge, Yield

Praise—Enter his gates with thanksgiving and his courts with praise. Sit quietly and thank God for who he is and what he has done for you. Find your place of peace and open your mouth by praising him for loving you, and then thank him for your life. Let everything that has breath praise the Lord.

Repent—This is where you take the things you did wrong and ask God for forgiveness. There is nothing that you have done that God does not already know about. He wants to hear them from you, so he knows you know they were wrong. Do not spend a lot of your time here; it is not meant to fill one of the Great Lakes up in one sitting. It is basically one wrong per request then repeat.

Acknowledge—Acknowledge that you are sorry for what you have done, and he is just for forgiving your sins. Believing that what has been done on the cross no longer has a hold on you.

Yield—As you build up your faith and yield to the Holy Spirit, he will show you things to pray, and people to pray for, and the way you should go. This is the part when you get still and listen as God does all the talking.

Let us then approach God's throne of grace with confidence, so that we may receive mercy and find grace to help us in our time of need. (Hebrews 4:16, NIV)

Prayer is communicating with God. It is twofold: listening and talking to him. Those who believe in God can pray from the heart in their own words or spontaneously by their heavenly language. It does not have to be eloquent; it just has to be honest. Do not let a moment, life event, or circumstances go by without first going to prayer.

In the beginning of this step, we gave you a scripture that shows you how to prepare yourself by putting on the armor of God. Once you believe in God and that he alone can deliver you out of the muddy waters, take a step of faith and enter his court.

Your intimacy with God will grow deeper as you take the time to talk with him each day. The more time you spend with him, the more you will get to know him. You will learn to become more intentional as you approach the throne of God and make it the most important conversation of the day. Just think about it: we are talking about you sitting on the lap of the Creator of the universe who is there for you, cares about you, and will listen with an ear to respond to your life, both for his glory and for your good. As you spend time with God, you will learn how to prayerfully give consideration to daily Bible readings then reflect upon what you have read and how the Lord has led you through the course of life.

Here is a sample prayer:

Father God, thank you for this day. Thank you that I get to enter into your court with an open heart and an open mind. Thank you for loving me and sending your son to die on the cross so I may live. I praise your holy name. I thank you for loving me enough to not let me die. I am sorry I did not believe in you when they told me about you years ago. I was only looking at the things of this world and not on the things in heaven. I can see that you are who they say you are. I can feel you are never-ending love in my heart. I can see your true existence throughout your word and on this earth. I yield myself to the Holy Spirit to show me where I went wrong and how to correct it. What to say and when not to say anything. I love you God, and may my hope be built on nothing less than Jesus's blood and his righteousness. Amen!

How often should you pray? Daily!

Now go put this truth into practice! God's word does not come back void. Get on your knees and cry out to Jesus. Believe that he came to set the captives free and has made you free. Free from the addictive behaviors. Free from your past. Free from your enemies. Free indeed!

How do you see yourself?

On the road to freedom!

Step 12

I have found a body of believers to fellowship with and call my home.

> *And let us consider one another in order to stir up love and good works. Not forsaking the assembling of ourselves together, as is the manner of some, but exhorting one another, and so much the more as you see the day approaching.* (Hebrews 10:24–25)

> *Do not be unequally yoked together with unbelievers. For what fellowship has righteousness with lawlessness? And what communion has light with darkness?* (2 Corinthians 6:14)

> *But if we walk in the light as He is in the light, we have fellowship with one another, and the blood of Jesus Christ His Son cleanses us from all sin.* (1 John 1:7)

Fellowship in the *Webster's New World Dictionary[1]* is

1. companionship; friendly association
2. a mutual sharing, as of experience, activity, interest, etcetera.
3. a group of people with the same interests; company; brotherhood...

So Christian fellowship is more than attending church; it is "assimilating" into the body of believers, becoming one in worshiping, loving, caring, and sharing. According to scripture, fellowship is not an optional matter for believers.

Not that we want to put any more emphasis on any one step, but AFL believes this is a key to the growth of your salvation and Christian walk. Like we said before, you cannot do this alone. Plus it is walking out in obedience according to scripture. You are not joining a church because it is a good place to grow spiritually. You join a local church because it is the expression of what Christ has made you into—a member of the body of Christ. Being united to Christ means being united to every Christian. Like a family! When you were born, you did not just become part of someone's family—you became part of their DNA. You took on the last name, bloodline, and everything else that goes with it—good or bad!

What happens a lot of times is someone gets offended at someone and wants to leave the church. God has not called us for separation but to be united with the body of believers. That is why he tells us to let our petitions be known. Again, good, or bad! We want you to take a hold of this step right out of the chute. Take a hold of the rope, wrap it around your hand nice and tight, and not let go until the bull comes to a stop. When you find a body of believers and they are strong in the word, do not leave just because someone told you that you are sitting in their seat. Just get up and find a new one and bless them on the way.

There are thousands of churches out there, and not all of them are good. Some of them are preaching their own understanding of what the word says. You need to find one that is preaching what the word of God says. If you are reading the word for yourself, you will be able to tell after the first few times of being there. The Holy Spirit will confirm it to you. When he does, run as fast as you can without looking back. You most likely will run into another one at the next corner. We say this with a joking attitude, but it is as serious as a heart attack.

AFL wants to point out that the size of the church does not always mean it is a good or bad church. We have seen a church with as few as ten people as a tabernacle of praise and a smorgasbord of the word, and we saw a church with thousands of members but is so dry that you can fall asleep during the worship time. Again, get in the word, and the Holy Spirit will confirm.

Talking about worship—worship is not just the beginning of a service where you might sing three songs and then sit down for the message. Worship starts from the time you get up until you go back to bed, and everything in between. Worship is the highest form of praise, and it is not for us, it is for God (AFL version). The Greek word for worship is latreuō (pronounced lat-ryoo'-o), and it means "to minister to God." Here is what *Merriam-Webster's Collegiate Dictionary*[2] says:

: the act of showing respect and love for a god especially by praying with other people who believe in the same god.
: the act of worshiping God or a god
: excessive admiration for someone.

Worship is giving God the respect he so deserves with every fiber of your being. In his book *How to Worship a King*, Zach Neese goes in further detail about true worship and how the old English word for worship was *worth-ship*. "It literally means to give something worth- to demonstratively attribute value, especially to a deity or god. It is easy to remember—we worth-ship God by communicating and demonstrating his value...If worship is ascribing worth to God, then the price of our worship shows God and the world how much we value him."[3]

In the book of John, Jesus was having a conversation with a Samaritan woman at the well (John 4:6–30). In the conversation, the woman was discussing places of worship with Jesus, saying that the Jews worshiped at Jerusalem while the Samaritans worshiped at Mount Gerizim. Jesus had just revealed that he knew about all of the many husbands she had in the past as well as the fact that the current man she was living with was not her husband. This made her uneasy, so she tried to divert his attention from her personal life to religion. Jesus refused to be distracted from his teaching on true worship and got to the heart of the matter: *"But the hour is coming, and now is, when the true worshipers shall worship the Father in spirit and truth, for the Father seeks such to worship Him"* (John 4:23).

The main teaching he was trying to convey is, worshiping the Lord in spirit and truth, God is not to be confined to a single church or act. With the coming of Christ, all of God's children gained equal access to God through him. Worship became a matter of the heart, not external actions, and directed by truth rather than ceremony. So to put it in a different way: to give of one's self in all areas of one's life.

Volunteering is a great way to worship the Lord. You are giving of yourself so others can feast. There is not a church on the planet that can function properly without volunteers. In some churches, the congregations think that the pastor is the most important person in their church when in fact it is the volunteers. We know of a church that has over thirty thousand members and over five thousand volunteers throughout multiple campuses. Who do you think is the most important person? There is no way the pastor can take care of thirty thousand people and live. If he had to pay for all the people to take care of five buildings with setup and cleaning, administrative, flyers and anything else that may be needed, there would not be enough money left over to feed the sheep.

Not even Moses could handle his priesthood with millions of Israelites. We want to share with you a long scripture to show you our point. Exodus chapter 18:1–27:

> *Now Jethro, the priest of Midian and father-in-law of Moses, heard of everything God had done for Moses and for his people Israel, and how the Lord had brought Israel out of Egypt.*
>
> *After Moses had sent away his wife Zipporah, his father-in-law Jethro received her and her two sons. One son was named Gershom, for Moses said, "I have become a foreigner in a foreign land"; and the other was named Eliezer, for he said, "My father's God was my helper; he saved me from the sword of Pharaoh.*
>
> *Jethro, Moses' father-in -law, together with Moses' sons and wife, came to him in the wilderness, where he was camped near the mountain of God. Jethro had sent word to him, "I, your father-in-law Jethro, am coming to you with your wife and her two sons.*
>
> *So Moses went out to meet his father-in-law and bowed down and kissed him. They greeted each other and then went into the tent. Moses told his father-in-law about everything the Lord had done to Pharaoh and the Egyptians for Israel's sake and about all the hardships they had met along the way and how the Lord had saved them. Jethro was delighted to hear about all the good things the Lord had done for Israel in rescuing them from the hand of the Egyptians. He said, "Praise be to the Lord, who rescued you from the hand of the Egyptians and of Pharaoh, and who rescued the people from the hand of the Egyptians. Now I know that the Lord is greater than all other gods, for he did this to those who had treated Israel arrogantly." Then Jethro, Moses' father-in -law, brought a burnt offering and other sacrifices to God, and Aaron came with all the elders of*

Israel to eat a meal with Moses' father-in-law in the presence of God.

The next day Moses took his seat to serve as judge for the people, and they stood around him from morning till evening. When his father-in-law saw all that Moses was doing for the people, he said, "What is this you are doing for the people? Why do you alone sit as judge, while all these people stand around you from morning till evening?

Moses answered him, "Because the people come to me to seek God's will. Whenever they have a dispute, it is brought to me, and I decide between the parties and inform them of God's decrees and instructions.

Moses' father-in-law replied, "What you are doing is not good. You and these people who come to you will only wear yourselves out. The work is too heavy for you; you cannot handle it alone. Listen now to me and I will give you some advice, and may God be with you. You must be the people's representative before God and bring their disputes to him. Teach them his decrees and instructions, and show them the way they are to live and how they are to behave. But select capable men from all the people— men who fear God, trustworthy men who hate dishonest gain—and appoint them as officials over thousands, hundreds, fifties and tens. Have them serve as judges for the people at all times, but have them bring every difficult case to you; the simple cases they can decide themselves. That will make your load lighter, because they will share it with you. If you do this and God so commands, you will be able to stand the strain, and all these people will go home satisfied.

Moses listened to his father-in-law and did everything he said. He chose capable men from all Israel and made them leaders of the people, officials over thousands, hundreds, fifties and tens. They served as judges for the

25

people at all times. The difficult cases they brought to Moses, but the simple ones they decided themselves.

Then Moses sent his father-in-law on his way, and Jethro returned to his own country." (Exodus 18:1– 27, NIV).

So with that being said, go get involved with your church and do it with all of your heart. Be there when you are scheduled and be on time. Look your best. Do not do it grudgingly but with the biggest smile any Christian could have. You are the light of the world, so let it shine!

One last time:

How do you see yourself?

Are you on the road to freedom?

Chapter 5

Living an Addictive Free Life

In a world where addiction is made out to be an incurable disease, it is hard to imagine living an addictive free life. There are programs for every addiction imaginable, but hardly any of them offer freedom. In some cases, people are given the opportunity to get their act together only to see that the work to stay clean is too hard. They give up hope and return to the life they once lived. The percentage in them getting the help they need at that point starts to decline and lowers every time they try. It is amazing all the information that can be found on the Internet along with the statistics that will boggle your mind. This is mainly because people are trying to work at getting free from addiction rather than living by faith.

There are addicts who were given the choice to walk away from their addiction but did not know how to cope with life, so they said no. Going away for a few days, weeks, or even months can look promising, but what happens when you need to return to society? One might ask themselves,

- How am I going to live without getting high?

- How can I go out to dinner and not eat all I want?

- What happens to the relationships I had; will they forgive me?

- How can I face my parents and family knowing I was into porn?

- Will I ever find a husband/wife if they know I was a porn star/prostitute?

- How can I go to a party and not get drunk?

- I love playing cards; will I ever be able to play for fun?

- I am in prison, why should it matter?

This list can get very lengthy on just the questions we have heard. What is your question? No matter what your question or concern is, you can live life openly and honestly. You can live in forgiveness, which starts with yourself. Once people start to see that you have forgiven yourself, they will follow suit. If for some reason they do not, that is okay too. Just keep forgiving yourself; it is not about what they think but how God thinks about you.

Essentially, living addictive free means living free. No more hidden lies, deception, stealing, conning to get what you want. Exposing everything! Living free from addiction means you will work and save to get what you want. Manage your money and time. Pay your bills and pay them on time. Watch how you speak. Make your bed and wash your clothes. Brush your teeth and wash your body. Watch what you eat and exercise. Number one is to stay healthy.

A healthy mind means a healthy body. You basically have to renew your mind, as found in Ephesians 4:22–32:

That you put off, concerning your former conduct, the old man which grows corrupt according to the deceitful lusts, and be renewed in the spirit of your mind, and that you put on the new man which was created according to

God, in true righteousness and holiness. Therefore, putting away lying, "Let each one of you speak truth with his neighbor," for we are members of one another. "Be angry, and do not sin": do not let the sun go down on your wrath, nor give place to the devil. Let him who stole steal no longer, but rather let him labor, working with his hands what is good, that he may have something to give him who has need. Let no corrupt word proceed out of your mouth, but what is good for necessary edification, that it may impart grace to the hearers. And do not grieve the Holy Spirit of God, by whom you were sealed for the day of redemption. Let all bitterness, wrath, anger, clamor, and evil speaking be put away from you, with all malice. And be kind to one another, tenderhearted, forgiving one another, even as God in Christ forgave you.

This holds true even if you are in an institution. Do not think that just because you are confined within some walls, you do not have to adhere to these principles. You will still have to answer to God for how you live your life once you have been told the truth. Reading this guidebook has placed you on a victory lap. Are you going to finish the race or give up?

You will need to change your old habits for godly ones. You will need to go back and work the steps found in the last chapter. Do not just work them with your flesh; use prayer as your foundation. Know who you are and make a decision to change it. One of our suggestions is accountability— finding someone who will mentor you and help you work the program. This will be someone that you can go to if you have any questions or you just need to talk out your problems. It is also suggested that you make no big life changes without first discussing it with your accountability partner because bad decisions that lead to failure can be triggers of old behaviors.

The way to overcome the results of a series of bad choices is through a series of right choices, and sometimes, you will need to do this with someone else. The only way to walk out of trouble is to do the opposite of whatever you did to get into trouble—one choice at a time and not alone. You cannot make a series of bad choices that result in significant problems and then make one good choice and expect all the results of all those bad choices to go away; that is why you need to seek help. You did not get into deep trouble through one bad choice; you got into trouble through a series of bad choices. You cannot do anything about what is behind you, but you can do a great deal about what lies ahead of you. God is a Redeemer, and he will always give you another chance.

In the workbook, you will be able to write out any questions or concerns you may have and then seek out the answers to them.

Chapter 6

What Happens if I Fall?

In one of the twelve-step programs, they state that relapse is a reality. It is not a reality; relapse is a choice, and you should never be forced into it. Once you make the decision to follow Christ and lay down the addiction, it no longer belongs to you; therefore it does not have to have control over your life. But sometimes it happens, and that is why AFL does not condemn you.

> *[Healing for the Backslider] And one shall say, "Heap it up! Heap it up! Prepare the way, Take the stumbling block out of the way of My people.* (Isaiah 57:14)

Very simply put, get back up and move on. Do not wallow in your mistake but instead lift yourself back up, brush yourself off, and know that you are not alone. You are not the first person to fall from your newfound way of life. Jesus is the only one who has ever stood on the path of righteousness without a fall or two. Do not allow self -pity to overtake your mind with thoughts like *See you cannot do it, I knew you were a failure...Oh well, since you are down, why do not you just stay here! You are a loser, and you just proved it!*

God loves you, and so do we. It does not matter that you fell; what matters is that you are willing to pick yourself back up and move forward. Remember, you are not in this alone, and sometimes we all need support to help us walk. In Hebrews 13:5, God says he will never leave us nor forsake us. Or in other words, he will never abandon us and leave us high and dry, or in your case, a pit. Jesus never fails; therefore if you hold on to him you will never fall totally away.

In Psalm 40:2, it says that God brought us out of a horrible pit, out of the miry clay, and set our feet upon a rock and established our goings. This is not just a one-time deal. He knows we fall short of the full glory of himself and is there for us over and over again. If you decide to abandon ship, God will never abandon you. This is why you cannot feel sorry for yourself because sorrow will stop the flow of what is good and what is pure.

You will need to go back to step 1 and look at why you chose to go back to the addiction. Was it because you left a door open and wasn't honest with yourself? Was it because the urge was greater than your desire to walk this out in freedom? Was it because of the people you were with? Only you can answer these questions and search for the right answers on how to not repeat them again. This is what is called insanity, doing the same things, and expecting different results.

Sometimes this could happen months or even years after laying down your addiction. You might feel badly shaken and more horrible than when you first started. We here at AFL would hope this is not the case because in some cases, relapse can be fatal. There is nothing sadder than to see someone make it to freedom and never get to walk out all that there is for them victoriously.

One of the greatest scriptures is Psalm 84:10: *"Better is one day in your courts than a thousand days elsewhere."* It is better to be in the presence of righteousness than evildoers. This guidebook, meetings, your church family—any one of them can make a difference in your decisions. Do not take them for granted. Sometimes when we get too comfortable with not having the addiction rule our lives, we might forget that we ever had a problem. This then puts us with people, at places, and around things that can lead us into thinking we can handle small amounts of our old way, thinking this time it will be different.

- I know where I went wrong, so I can control it.

- I will only have one drink.

- I will only do one line.

- I will only play one game, and whether I lose or win, I will walk away.

- I will only have one bag of chips instead of three.

One of the things with laying our addiction down is that we are willing to never pick it back up again. We are to forgive ourselves and know that God has forgiven us, but we are never to forget the pain it caused us. Many of us are walking as overcomers, glorifying in victory, but we will never look back and say, "They were the good old days. I think I want to return to my slop and taste it to see if it tastes the same." No! God forbid, it is not any different today than it was last week, last month, or even twenty years ago. "We remember!"

Don't be like 2 Peter 2:22 in the Amplified: *"There has befallen them the thing spoken of in the true proverb. The dog turns back to his own vomit, and, The sow is washed only to wallow again in the mire."* Proverbs 26:11, in the Amplified, says it this way: *"As a dog returns to his vomit, so a fool returns to his folly."*

It is important for you to share with your accountability person the feelings of using or your behavior attitudes. Many new folks think it is really abnormal for an addict to want to get high or a person who has trouble with other addictions to want to continue doing what they may have done for years. Then when we feel these old urges rising up in us, we think there is something wrong and we have the tendency to beat ourselves up. The desire to go back will pass, but only if you work through them. Eventually, these appetites or thoughts will lessen, and you will be moving forward.

Do not isolate yourself from AFL, your church, or any home meetings you have found help in, because isolation is an extremely dangerous place and will stump your spiritual growth. You need to keep yourself surrounded by people who love you and know what you are going through. People who will have mercy with your character defects and will be honest with you in helping you change and grow in the word.

Many of us have messed up in our lives, and through repentance, we have seen that God's grace is always willing to receive us back with open arms, in love and mercy. We all need God!

Now go to the workbook to write down a statement of confession that you will try your best not to fall, but if you do that, you will not condemn yourself.

Chapter 7

Recovery vs. Deliverance

In a world that says that addictions are incurable, it is hard to wrap one's brain around the fact that this statement is not so. We have been misinformed for so many years that it has altered the mind in the way that people think about addictions. We are here to show, with the help of the gospel, that statement to be inaccurate. There is plenty of evidence, both inside the word and outside, to show that God has delivered people with addictions. They have claimed that addictions are hereditary; yes, this might be true. They have claimed that once an addict always an addict—yes, in the world system, this might be true. But in most cases, it is the mind that has changed and that has people making statements like "I cannot stop…I don't know how to get through this…Every time I try to stop, I just end up right back where I was." Whatever the cause may be, once a mind has changed and a person starts to use or do something differently, like eat or drink too much for example, that person experiences hopelessness. Yes, we have the chemical imbalance in the body that makes it harder to stop, but that does not make it impossible to stop. Once you become clean—or stop using, or stop doing, or stop eating—for a period, the mind can be changed back to its original form.

Here is a quote from a picture the author has hanging in his office with the caption about *focus*: "Change your thoughts and you change your world" (Norman Vincent Peale).

Let us just touch base on drugs for a second. Why are so many of them called a mind-mood-altering substance? Because they change the mind into a mood that was not the original setting it was made to be. So here you will need to work with the word of God to put the word of God back in your mind to change it into the mind-mood-altering Word. You will need to change the mind back to "Yes, I can," that is why you've got to take a hold of the scripture "I can do all things through Christ who strengthens me" (Philippians 4:13). You have power over all of your thoughts once you become a child of God. You inherited the same power that was given to Jesus by God, and that gives you the authority to speak over your situation. You have the power to command the addiction to be gone from you! You have the authority to start to change your mind! You change your mind, you see deliverance.

In other twelve-step programs, when they tell you to keep coming back, you are going back to what you were each time. In God, in this twelve-step program, we stand on where you are going, not where you came from. Deliverance is being set free from what was. The word of God puts the claim on what will be. You have been delivered! Jesus took the addiction on the cross for you, now all you need to do is to stand with that claim, believe it, and it shall be yours. Proclaim it with your mouth, and it will come to pass. AFL is not here to say that this will work for everybody, even though we believe it could. It will only work for those that honestly believe. It will only work for those who truly stand on faith. This guidebook was written with the hope that all those that read it will grab ahold of the truth and will want the freedom from the addiction.

We would like to mention again that when we talk about addictions, we are grouping all of them together. When we talk about a person who can't stop going to the casinos having the same mind-set of a person who can't stop going to the bar, of a person who can't stop putting a needle in their arm, of a person who can't stop smoking marijuana, of a person who can't stop lying, of a person who can't stop stealing, of a person who can't stop eating—we are saying that all kinds of substances leads to the same mind -set results. The only difference between each one of them is what it does chemically to the body: overeating, too much sugar; over gambling, too much debt; overdrinking, cirrhosis of the liver; too many drugs, brain damage. One of the things we like to look at in the difference between recovery and deliverance is recovery is putting a Band-Aid on an open sore; you may put some type of ointment on it to help it heal, but the scaring will always be there. Deliverance is having it attended by a physician that will clean the inside, stitch it, seal it, and almost make it new with only a very minimum amount of scarring. Though you may look at it and still see that there was an injury there, but the difference between the two is one will always be noticeable and the other will go away.

Here is another analogy we like to consider with the difference between recovery and deliverance: Let's say you are standing on a street corner, and it is raining (in some of your situations it will be a drizzle and in others pouring). Recovery would be when someone comes by and hands you an umbrella. It works but it is not complete. Your legs are still getting soaked and your feet are still drenched. Deliverance would be when someone comes by and they open up the door to their vehicle and you step in, completely out from the rain. Complete with a heater to dry you off so that very soon, there is no evidence you were even in the rain.

Recovery, according to *Merriam-Webster's Collegiate Dictionary*[1] is

: the act or process of becoming healthy after an illness or injury.
: the act or process of recovering.
: the act or process of returning to a normal state after a period of difficulty: the process of combating a disorder (as alcoholism) or a real or perceived problem: the return of something that has been lost, stolen, etcetera.

Deliverance, according to *Webster's Dictionary of the English Language*[2] is "liberation from bondage or rescue from danger."

In other words, *deliverance* is getting rid of the junk in your life. It is yours and yours alone and cannot be shared with anyone else. That is why in chapter 4 the steps are the "Twelve I Haves," not the twelve "we haves." We did not put you in the situation you are in, it was you who did. You may think it was because of your circumstances, but it really was your decision, not the circumstances. Therefore it is you who has to take the first step. Once you have worked through the twelve steps in chapter 4, you can be assured that God has delivered you. God is the author of life and you have the authority, which is given by him, to tell the addiction to leave. When our lives reflect the word, we will walk in the authority.

One of the biggest differences of recovery and deliverance is one keeps you in bondage and the other sets you free. When you are in recovery, you are always looking over your shoulders to see how you are doing. You are always wondering if you will ever stop thinking about the addiction and for the urge to go away. As the *Merriam-Webster Collegiate Dictionary* says, it is the process of combating a disorder (as alcoholism) or any other addictive behavior. When you are walking in deliverance according to the word of God, you are free from the addiction and no longer need to look over your shoulders, and the word will help you renew your mind so that the memory will become less and less as you walk out this type of recovery.

If we are to believe that the word of God is true and that every word in the Bible has a meaning, then we have to believe that God leans more on deliverance than he does on recovery. In the NKJV Bible, there are only three verses that mention recovery; however there are ninety-eight verses that talk about deliverance. Remember the word *deliverance*, because the difference between being clean and sober—in other words abstinence—and true recovery is in a process called deliverance, something only found in Jesus. There are many formulas or words used to present the process, which are available to assist in the process of recovery; but there is only one way to deliverance, and his name is Jesus.

That is why AFL focuses on deliverance in the sense of letting God remove the addiction from you so that he, and only him, can fill you up with the power and strength to overcome the addiction. Once you overcome the addiction, you can fulfill the recovery process according to the Webster Dictionary and live a healthier life. Deliverance is a one-time act but a lifelong process of being changed and conformed more and more to the image of God.

AFL wants to make sure that you understand that just because you get free from the addiction, it does not mean that everything is going to be perfect in your life. You will still come against adversity and run into a hurdle or two or three or four. The only difference is this time, when you run into them, you will know where to go for help, and in some cases, know how to get over them on your own and not turn toward the addiction to cover it up.

Chapter 8

Vision

Where there is no vision [no redemptive revelation of God], the people perish; but he who keeps the law [of God, which includes that of man]—blessed (happy, fortunate, and enviable) is he. (Proverbs 29:18, AMP)

The word *vision*, used here, has to do with the word of God. "Where there is no word of God, where there is no message of life, the people perish" is the primary interpretation of this passage. We want to use this vision (word of God) to help you gain your vision, and that is why we included this scripture as this chapter's reference. We think that it speaks of another kind of vision—a work of God in the hearts of men and women. The part of being blessed (happiness) is the by-product of holiness and faithfulness rather than the main objective in and of itself.

Today life is good. Today life is worth living. Today in my addiction-free world, life is love (Anthony Ordille)[1]

Have you ever used a GPS? The map might have a balloon, sign, or some type of symbol pointing out the position of where you are currently. This is fine if you are looking to see where you are, but the whole purpose of a GPS system is to guide you to a place you do not know how to get to. So in essence, the You Are Here sign is a symbol of where you are going from where you are. Now just replace the sign's wording with the word *vision*. Vision is where you are going from where you are now.

The *Merriam-Webster's Collegiate Dictionary*[2] says vision is

: the ability to see; sight or eyesight.
: something that you imagine; a picture that you see in your mind.
: something that you see or dream especially as part of a religious or supernatural experience.

In order for you to walk in your newfound life, you will have to have a vision. In other words, you will need a plan. Everything up to now most likely was not working for you, and the path you were on was leading you to the destruction that is at hand. Obviously, this is not where you want to be, or you would not be looking to overcome your past. You will need to spend some time reviewing what your objectives are and how you are going to get there. It will be like writing a résumé for a job and selling yourself. It is imperative for you to pursue the heart of God daily in order to stay focused with the task at hand. You must seek God's heart to obtain clarity for your future to stay clear of the addiction. If you do not keep looking forward, you will end right back where you came from. You must also have a sense of what God has called you to do for him and his church.

The more time you spend in prayer with God, the clearer your vision will become. Sometimes the cares of this world can cloud up your vision, and what appeared to be right was five degrees off the target, and you end up at the wrong place. That is why AFL focuses on hearing from God rather than man because God's ways are always clear! That is also why we do not express it as dreams. Saying something like "What is your dream?"—that statement is too vague. Vision is more like setting something in play until you get there, and a dream is something that you are hoping for but might not work toward it.

Once you put your vision down on paper, you will have to put it to work in order to accomplish it. *"And the Lord answered me and said, Write the vision and engrave it so plainly upon tablets that everyone who passes may [be able to] read [it easily and quickly] as he hastens by"* (Habakkuk 2:2, AMP).

Vision is like looking at your life from the Hubble Space Telescope. The Hubble must maintain a steady position in space, and its primary mirror must remain in proper focus at all times. With this illustration, we can say that the primary mirror you need is God. If you keep him in line with your vision, he will keep the focus that is needed to reach your destiny. Even though focus is your responsibility, proper focus requires a consistent yearning for God in every area of your life. Your thoughts must be centered on him and your passions converge with his. Keep your eye fixed on him, and when you see the future, it would be without question.

Outside of the vision in Proverbs 29:18, Solomon talks about the law of God, which includes that of man. The law of God is simple for people to understand because we always relate to that as the Ten Commandments. Solomon includes the law of man as part of the vision. So as you review what your plan is, make sure to include obeying "What is Caesar's belongs to Caesar." In other words, obey the laws of the land! If you were a thief, stop stealing. If you were not paying your income taxes, start paying them. If you were a liar, tell the truth from now on. Do you get the picture?

We can say that this all boils down to setting goals— short
-term goals, just-over-the -horizon goals, and long-term goals.
Never make any major decisions without first going to God in
prayer and talking it over with your spiritual leader.

Short-term goals will be something like "Just for today, I
am going to stay clean, or not eat the whole cake, or not go to
the casino," or stay away from whatever addictive behavior you
may have. "Just for today I am going to go to work and give
110 percent all day long and do things before they ask me to do
them."

Just-over-the-horizon goals are goals that will get you
through the next few weeks and months and can be something
like "I will not miss a day of work. I will pay my bills on time
this month, I will bring my lunch to work this week, I will spend
time with my family instead of going to the bar," or any other
change that may be needed.

Long-term goals can be something on the lines of going
back to school to get a degree so you can get a higher-paying
job, buying a house, or even moving to a different apartment,
getting married, or starting a family. Some call this the five-to-
ten-year plan. Again, never make a major decision without
seeking God's approval and talking it over with a spiritual
leader. Make sure this is someone who hears from God. This is
so you know that it is not a diversion from the devil or even
your own self. Sometimes you can make decisions thinking it
is the right one when in fact you are trying to sabotage a good
thing. It was your nature to just be spontaneous on doing things
without thinking. Now it is time to do them from a mature
perspective and not from the hurt emotions.

Goals, when they are rooted in scripture, can be a helpful
way of motivating yourself so that they become reachable.

See a list of scriptures in section 3 under "Vision/ Revelation" that will help you grow in this area. Use the workbook to write down your vision statement so that you can keep it in front of you and read it whenever you need encouragement.

Chapter 9

Praying for Others

Therefore I exhort first of all that supplications, prayers, intercessions, and giving of thanks be made for all men. (2 Timothy 2:1)

And pray in the Spirit on all occasions with all kinds of prayers and requests. With this in mind, be alert and always keep on praying for all the Lord's people. (Ephesians 6:18, NIV)

After you get cleaned up from the addiction, hopefully you will grow in your faith; and just like a bird has to leave its nest, you will begin to start to pray for others. This is why we added this chapter to the guidebook, to help you learn some key elements on how to pray for others—even though there are a great number of teachings out there that give more in-depth information.

Even though God is the real teacher, we lay out just a few basic concepts to help you understand how to pray. It does not matter whether you are a new Christian or have been one for years—when you are ready to get serious about your prayer life, God is there to help. Ask him to guide and strengthen you.

When praying, pray what the word says, not your feelings. You have to learn to be submissive to God's will, just like Jesus did. You have to turn your heart to hearing what the Father says and pray it out, sometimes in a heavenly language. You will have to model Jesus's characteristic of the prayer if you are to be conformed to his likeness.

Talking about a heavenly language: You may be asking yourself, what do they mean by that? There are a lot of teachings about this. Some say that it is not for today, that it was only in the Old Testament. Some teach that it needs to be prayed for and God will give it to you if you believe hard enough. The Bible says that when a person asks Jesus into their heart, they are a new creation and all things have passed away and the Holy Spirit is instantly in them and a heavenly language is given to them right then. In another way when you accept Jesus, the Trinity—Father, Son, Holy Spirit—all find their way into your heart, and they intertwine with your spirit. Therefore when we say you can pray in a heavenly language, that means that the Holy Spirit, who lives in you right from the start, will pray to the Father exactly what needs to be prayed.

Speaking in your heavenly language bypasses the mind—carnal thinking—and speaks directly from the spirit to the throne room of God without any interruption or interference from the world. So when we say to pray in the spirit, we are clearly saying God is speaking to himself. It is a person's desire to use it that allows it to come out of the mouth. No one can pray for someone and make them speak in the spirit. You will have to say something like "Father, I accept your spirit, I accept the ability to be able to speak in the spirit. Amen!"

The characteristic of Jesus was obedient to what he heard the Father say, and he did what he had seen the Father do. He talks about this in John 5: 19–20: *"Then Jesus answered and said to them, 'Most assuredly, I say to you, the Son can do nothing of Himself, but what He sees the Father do; for whatever He does, the Son also does in like manner. For the Father loves the Son, and shows Him all things that He Himself does; and He will show Him greater works than these, that you may marvel.'"* Just because he was here on earth does not mean he automatically got it. He had to learn obedience, submission, passion and compassion, and victory. He offered up prayers and petitions with loud cries and tears. That is why you have to spend time with him to become familiar with his voice (John 10:27).

It is through the heartfelt prayers that God answers! What or who is in your heart? Your country? A family member? The upcoming election? A lost loved one? The most effective prayers are when you pray from the heart.

You may be asking yourself, "Why do I need to pray?" The answer to that question is quite simple: because prayer binds you to God, and he uses it to develop you. He uses it to give direction on how you are to stand in battle against the evil that is in this world. When you pray, you experience fellowship; you become a worker together with Him (2 Corinthians 6:1). When you pray, God gives you the enjoyment and privilege of administrating his kingdom, his affairs working together with Him. He could do it without you, but you cannot do it without Him. When you pray, God is growing you. God never wants you to live independent of Him. If God just did everything for you and you never had to pray, soon you would begin to take things for granted; you would cease to depend upon God.

You are part of the body of believers, and as a whole, we are his hands, feet, and voice to help build the church. Do not think of prayer as a necessity—even a requirement. Just like having a driving license is a privilege to drive here in America, so is praying for others. It is as if God has made a way for you to be on the honor roll of life—it is an honor to pray his word and see it manifest. If you are reading this book and/or you have accepted Christ into your heart, you got here because someone prayed for you. Oh, what glory that God allows us the privilege of doing it with Him!

One of the things you need to be careful with is settling into a routine that comes with a mental checklist: so many people and concerns to pray about! It will help you not to slip into that kind of thinking if you focus on the real purpose and privilege of your prayer life. Prayer is not something you have to do; it is something you get to do. It is a mind-set that can give you a whole new approach to prayer.

There will be times that things will happen to cause your prayer life to slow down or even cease; do not slip into guilt. Instead, pick it back up as soon as you can, but hopefully, it does not stop for good. It is a good idea to develop a quiet time to read the Bible or daily devotional. Pray as you can during the day—in the car, walking, cleaning house—any time your mind is free.

Daily Quiet Time:

The encouraging thing is that we can all begin with just a few minutes a day. Decide on a few personal guidelines for your prayer life:

- When to have it: (it can be whenever you are free, some say it is best first thing in the morning)

- How long to spend: (be realistic; God will honor even a few minutes a day if you are consistent)

- Where to have it: (somewhere private, undisturbed)

Out of all the scriptures that talk about prayer, there are none that say one will be condemned if they do not have a quiet time. There is, however, some guidelines— surrendering your will and time in the word. Putting these into action will establish the relationship between you and the Lord. It will set the foundation for prayer as you move through your day.

Begin by worshiping the Lord with thanksgiving, just like what we spoke about in step 11.

You can do a devotional Bible reading—initially it is a good idea to follow a plan that will take you through the entire Bible, even if it takes a year or more. Ask the Lord to help you understand and apply what you read.

Your quiet time can be as brief as ten to fifteen minutes, but if you want to grow in your relationship with the Lord and your understanding of prayer, it is essential that you find the discipline to be consistent. The best way to do that is to enlist God's help. He will take you from these beginning steps into depths of prayer you never dreamed possible. It just takes time my friend.

Do not babble. *"And when you pray, do not keep on babbling like pagans, for they think they will be heard because of their many words"* (Matthew 6:7). This type of prayer has no meaning! Robotic prayer would be words of repetition, requiring no thought, no concentration, or having no heart— words so familiar that your thoughts easily drift as you pray. That is the opposite of the "effective, fervent prayer" that James speaks of in James 5:16, *"Confess your trespasses to one another, and pray for one another, that you may be healed. The effective, fervent prayer of a righteous man avails much."* Certainly, we can pray for our loved ones every day without being vainly repetitious.

Effective prayer is prayer that is offered in the name of Jesus (John 14:12–14), in his authority, according to his nature and character, asking for what He would ask. It is prayer according to the will of the Father (1 John 5:14–15), which certainly includes praying scripture—prayers taken directly from the Bible, such as the beautiful prayers of the Apostle Paul or verses of scripture turned into prayers. You are on powerful praying ground when you pray God's word, whether spontaneous or with written prayers.

Your prayers do not have to be eloquent. It is not the length, or the type of words used that matters. It is the warmth, intensity of feelings, zeal of your heart—not emotions, but genuine love for God and for others that reaches the throne room. God's word tells us that though we look on the outside appearance of a person, God looks at the heart (1 Samuel 16:7). That is as true of prayer as any other part of life.

Every prayer you lift to God is a course of action against Satan. If you are praying effectively—especially as you seek the salvation of loved ones and friends—you must recognize that Satan, the devil, is your enemy. Peter writes, *"Be self-controlled and alert. Your enemy the devil prowls around like a roaring lion looking for someone to devour. Resist him, standing firm in the faith, because you know that your brothers throughout the world are undergoing the same kind of sufferings"* (1 Peter 5:8–9).

He is not an enemy to be taken lightly. Though he has been defeated in the shed blood of Jesus Christ on the cross, he is a powerful adversary who, by his trickery and deceit, continues to confuse those hearts that have not been fully yielded to Christ—who are not yet under the control of God's Holy Spirit—you might have been one of those people.

When you pray for others, you are entering into warfare. Spiritual warfare is doing battle with this crafty enemy. If you are to battle effectively, in prayer (which is the only battlefield on which you can defeat him), you need to be aware of how he attracts and controls those who are his. One of his strategies is the spiritual stronghold.

What is a stronghold?

A stronghold is a well-fortified place; fortress. It is also a place where a particular cause or belief is strongly defended or upheld. This mainly takes place in one's mind. Satan cannot have your heart once you give it to God, but he can control the mind, or some will say the soul realm—mind, will, and emotion. A stronghold can be any mind-set that is contrary to God's word. Strongholds can be allowed by thoughts or feelings. They are built upon deception and error—which are from a wide variety of sources, including environment, peers, parents, or even demon spirits.

Other strongholds may be purely emotional or psychological. Much of modern psychology seeks to deal with *codependency*—a condition in which two people are drawn together in an attempt to meet their individual needs only to discover that together they find greater weakness, not strength. Whether physical, emotional, psychological, or spiritual in origin, strongholds are best defined as areas of bondage to Satan. The Bible describes Satan, his power, and how he uses it, and that clarifies what you should ask.

For instance, Jesus said Satan is the father of lies (John 8:46). How many lies would it take to keep someone out of God's will and away from the personal love relationship God wants with him?

Since strongholds are built upon error and falsehood, it is through the truth—word of God and prayer that you tear down such faulty thinking patterns.

For the weapons of our warfare are not carnal but mighty in God for pulling down strongholds. (2 Corinthians 10:4)

So when you are praying for someone that you know has a stronghold, and most of them do, you will need to pray a hedge of protection around their mind.

God will put a hedge of protection around his people so that the devil cannot touch them or all that they have. In the book of Job it gives us a clear picture:

Now there was a day when the sons of God came to present themselves before the Lord, and Satan also came among them. And the Lord said to Satan, "From where do you come?" So Satan answered the Lord and said, "From going to and fro on the earth, and from walking back and forth on it." Then the Lord said to Satan, "Have you considered My servant Job, that there is none like him on the earth, a blameless and upright man, one who fears God and shuns evil?" So Satan answered the Lord and said, "Does Job fear God for nothing? Have You not made a hedge around him, around his household, and around all that he has on every side? You have blessed the work of his hands, and his possessions have increased in the land. But now, stretch out Your hand and touch all that he has, and he will surely curse You to Your face!" And the Lord said to Satan, "Behold, all that he has is in your power; only do not lay a hand on his person." So Satan went out from the presence of the Lord." (Job 1:6–12)

Here is one of the best scriptures for safety of abiding in the presence of God:

He who dwells in the secret place of the Most High
Shall abide under the shadow of the Almighty.
I will say of the Lord, "He is my refuge and my
fortress; My God, in Him I will trust." Surely He shall
deliver you from the snare of the fowler and from the
perilous pestilence. He shall cover you with His
feathers,
And under His wings you shall take refuge;
His truth shall be your shield and buckler.
You shall not be afraid of the terror by night,
Nor of the arrow that flies by day,
Nor of the pestilence that walks in darkness,
Nor of the destruction that lays waste at noonday.
A thousand may fall at your side,
And ten thousand at your right hand;
But it shall not come near you.
Only with your eyes shall you look, And see the reward
of the wicked.
Because you have made the Lord, who is my refuge,
Even the Most High, your dwelling place,
No evil shall befall you,
Nor shall any plague come near your dwelling;
For He shall give His angels charge over you,
To keep you in all your ways.
In their hands they shall bear you up,
Lest you dash your foot against a stone.
You shall tread upon the lion and the cobra,
The young lion and the serpent you shall trample
underfoot. "Because he has set his love upon Me,
therefore I will deliver him;
I will set him on high, because he has known My name.
He shall call upon Me, and I will answer him;
I will be with him in trouble;
I will deliver him and honor him.
With long life I will satisfy him,
And show him My salvation. (Psalm 91)

Here is an example of a prayer:

Heavenly Father, I ask you to place a hedge of protection around (say their name here). To hide (say their name here) from the enemy, familiar spirits, wrongful thinking, making it impossible for any influence to have an effect on (say their name here). Send the right kind of friends in their life and keep them safe. Protect them from harm and watch over them. In Jesus's name!

You can also pray a hedge of thorns around them to protect them from friends who influence them in the wrong way. In prayer, you can set protective boundaries around the individuals, marriages, and families reached through your intercession.

When you intercede for those you love and ask the Lord to protect them from the evil one, how do you know what to pray? You turn to the word. First John 2:14 tells you how to pray for what a person needs to stand against Satan's lies: *"I write to you young men, because you are strong, and the word of God lives in you, and you have overcome the evil one."* You pray for the knowledge of the word of God to discern between Satan's lies and the truth.

You ask that your loved one would be led to spend time reading the Bible consistently every day, that they would find a Bible they readily understand, and they are comfortable with, that God would lead them to a church where the word of God is taught, that the Holy Spirit of truth would enlighten their understanding.

You would ask that the Lord help them to abide in the vine, to allow Jesus and his word to live in them—that the truth of scripture would be so much a part of them and that they could immediately spot one of Satan's lies. In all of this, you know you pray according to God's will and those are the prayers God promises to answer (1 John 5:14–15).

When you pray for others, it is a form of intercession. Intercession is interceding on someone else's behalf. When someone or something comes to mind, it is your opportunity to meet with God on their behalf in intercession.

Develop a prayer list.

Sometimes you may be overwhelmed with prayer request or desires to pray for others. Intercession needs to be part of your daily prayer life but does not need to be a chore. You might need to set some boundaries though: just because you are now in the position to pray for others does not mean you are at their every whim. You have to take care of yourself first, whether it be physical, emotional, or spiritual. Then you can set the time and place to go to the throne room on their behalf. There will be those times however, when God brings someone or something to mind, sometimes waking you up in the middle of the night, that you will have to obey and pray right then. When your King quickens your heart, you are to be ready to battle the enemy in prayer.

Know that you are not alone in this battle:

God is a wall of fire around you (Zechariah 2:5).

He surrounds you as the mountains surround Jerusalem (Psalm 125:2).

He is your Mighty Warrior (Jeremiah 20:11).

He is the Commander of the armies of heaven (Joshua 5:15).

Your Strong Tower (Psalm 61:3).

Your fortress (Psalm 31:3).

Your Stronghold (Psalm 43:2).

Your sure foundation (Isaiah 28:16), *the rock on which you stand* (Psalm 94:22).

Your Shepherd who protects and defends you (Psalm 23:1).

Your Most High God (Psalm 91:1).

You are indwelt by the spirit of supplication (Zechariah 12:10).

He is the Holy Spirit who lives in you and is your helper in prayer (Romans 8.26).

He is coming alongside you, and together the word gets connected with God. Paul is not saying in Romans 8:26 that you should throw up your hands when you do not know what to ask in prayer and just let the Spirit do it. He is saying when you are praying, the spirit helps you when you do not know what to ask. You must first do your part.

As you spend time with him, you will develop the ability to recognize his voice when he speaks to you by placing his thoughts into your mind and his desires into your heart.

How can you be sure such thoughts and desires are from him? Because Jesus promised we will know: *"The sheep listen to [the shepherd's] voice. He calls his own sheep by name and leads them out...his sheep follow him because they know his voice. But they will never follow a stranger; in fact, they will run away from him because they do not recognize a stranger's voice"* (John 10:2–5).

Note that the sheep had to listen, to be attentive and responsive. Sheep have to learn to recognize their shepherd's voice, as you learn to recognize the voice of any other person. The better you know someone, the easier that becomes. Jesus leaves no doubt—you will be able to recognize his voice—even though he speaks silently—if you are listening.

It is good to pray for others, even those you do not know, but sometimes it can be frustrating because you are not sure what to ask. We are told that if we pray according to God's will, we can have whatever we ask (1 John 5:14–15), but often prayer requests are for things in which we cannot be certain of his will.

If you are a person who develops a life of prayer and you enjoy praying for others, an intercessor, people will be drawn to you for prayer. It is wonderful to be able to intercede for others, but as requests increase, it can be difficult to find sufficient time to pray for them all.

Here are some manageable suggestions:

One way to keep from being overwhelmed with a growing list of prayer concerns is to pray immediately with a person asking for prayer. In person or on the phone, simply ask, "May I pray for you right now?" Keep in mind that this is only if your time allows it; do not be pressured into doing it right on the spot if you are pressed for time, like running late for work.

Maintaining an ongoing prayer list can be helpful for your daily prayers. Allow yourself to set a limit on the length of time you will pray for each request; otherwise, your list will just keep growing and may become unmanageable.

A good rule of thumb is to pray for each request for one month—a minimum of once a week. You can always pray more frequently as time allows, or for a longer period.

Keep your system simple. Add prayer requests to a weekly list that you keep in a small notebook or maybe even a prayer journal. You can even put a date to the requests. Begin a new list every week, dropping off the list any request that is more than four weeks old. Be sure to keep your inactive lists where you can find them, and periodically review them to note the answers you have seen. This exercise will build your faith!

One way to be sure you are praying God's will is to pray God's word. In practical terms, you can pray one prayer with verses from scripture over the entire list—scriptures that are clearly God's will for anyone, such as:

- that they will seek his kingdom and righteousness as a priority of life (Matthew 6:33),

- that they will know and follow him as their Shepherd (Psalm 23:1),

- that they will tithe and give generously (Malachi 3:10; Luke 6:38).

These verses are not only his will, but in context, they are linked to promises of provision for daily needs to be met. After praying such verses, knowing that in his timing and his way he will answer, you can comfortably move quickly through your list of names and requests without feeling the need to give God a lot of details. You can know you have already asked for things that are on his heart and he has promised to do.

When praying for an unsaved loved one or friend, this scripture prayer guide may be your key to victory. According to scripture, Jesus Christ came to seek and to save those who are lost. As his disciple, you are to join him in that dedication;

but when you have told them about the saving power of Jesus, and they have turned a deaf ear, what are you to do?

Your only power is that which is granted you by the Heavenly Father through his Holy Spirit. You can claim that power only through prayer. The Bible contains a full list of truths about your position in Christ and the ways of God regarding those who need his saving grace. It is your guide as you intercede for the lost.

Keep in mind that you have to pray the scriptures either by memory, reading them out loud, or even paraphrasing. To pray effectively for the lost, you must first learn to pray with your mind (1 Corinthians 14:15), deliberately thinking through and selecting specific verses. This truly is praying in the spirit (Ephesians 6:18) as you allow the Holy Spirit to bring his word to mind as you pray.

Here are a few verses you might select in your prayers for the lost. We have noted and paraphrased the verses. Use these scriptures as you pray specifically for your lost loved one or friend.

Affirming God's heart for the lost:

- He is not willing for anyone to perish (2 Peter 3:19)

- He wants all men to be saved (1 Timothy 2:13)

- Jesus gave himself as a ransom for all men (1 Timothy 2:5–6)

Acknowledging what you know to be true of the lost:

- They will not seek after God on their own (Romans 3:11)

- They cannot discern spiritual things (1 Corinthians 2:14)

- God alone can draw them to Jesus (John 6:40)

- God alone can enable them to come to Christ (John 6:65)

- They must be born again (John 1:13, 3:6–7)

We hope this chapter was helpful in giving you some understanding about praying for others. We also hope that the guidebook has been a blessing to you and that it has been effective with overcoming the addictive behavior you are facing. Please send us a note or a testimony to let us know if this program has been helpful, or if you have accepted Jesus Christ into your heart.

Please continue to section 2 to read a few of the many testimonies from people just like you who have overcome their addictive behavior by the compassion of Jesus Christ. Use section 3 to build yourself up anytime you need help.

May the Lord bless you and keep you;

May the Lord make His face shine upon you,
And be gracious to you;

May the Lord lift up His countenance upon you,
And give you peace

(Numbers 6:24–26)

Section 2

Testimonies

I have rejoiced in the way of your testimonies as much as in all riches.

—Psalm 119:14

In this section, you can read just some of the many testimonies from people who have been set free from their addictions. These are from a variety of addictions, but all have the same ending. They found their freedom from turning their will over to Jesus Christ.

They are printed as written.

The Secret *by Tim R*

Nobody wants to live with a secret, it torments your soul, and it bothers your conscience. I created this guy that everyone loved, and I went home and did not like myself. The effect of holding a secret that long is that you never have the freedom to be you. I do not carry secrets anymore.

One day, we were playing in the neighborhood. I grew up in a nice little neighborhood, just playing with some friends and there was this neighbor that lived across the street from me. He told me to come over to his house, so I went to his house and did not go inside the house; he said come into the garage I have to show you something. So I go into the garage and he just started touching me, just inappropriate touching. I was eight and I did not know what was going on. I did not know what he was doing, but I knew it was not right. I came home and I walked in the door and my mom asked me how my day was. That was the day I became a professional liar, and I got really good at it. A couple days later I got called to the garage again and again and again and yet again. I do not know how to process this, I do not know where to begin with this, I do not know how to deal with this, all I did know is if my dad found out he would kill him.

So I had to keep it a secret. I was literally becoming two different people—the guy that could go to school and get through the day, and then there be the guy that could not stop looking at pornography. This is not casual, I cannot stop! I am driven to this thing! So I had to keep it a secret. I do not know what to do with these questions that I have. I do not have answers for this. I am twelve, I am thirteen, I am fourteen, fifteen, sixteen, seventeen, eighteen years old. I am nineteen, and this thing is still on me. My mom caught me; I did not know what to say. I was embarrassed. I felt like a pervert. I felt completely disgusted with myself; because she is a praying woman, she went back to her room and started praying for me. It was probably the best prayer I think my mother has ever prayed. I did not hear it, but that prayer came and got me.

I got up, cleaned myself off, walk down the hallway. If I make a left I am going to my room and never talk about it again. If I make a right maybe I will have enough strength to go into her room and tell her what the real situation was, because it was not porn! That was not the root of the situation. I made a right and my mom cried, I cried, and then she went and got my younger brother. He came into the room and he said he got molested by the same guy. Then all three of us cried. My dad came home, we share what happened and then my mom says that she got sexually abused when she was six and then my dad said he got molested when he was five. So in one night my exposure caused everyone to come clean and confess their pain.

I mean that night, man, I just cannot articulate how good it felt to be able to tell the truth to somebody and not be judged. It is the most—oh my God, to have the truth come out and be surrounded by nothing but love. My parents' relationship with Christ is amazing; they have always been authentic and real on how they live out their faith. I just thank God that they were not the type of deep religious people that cannot handle pain. I was simply happy that they loved me, that they did not judge me. We did not grow up in an atmosphere where we saw any hypocrisy. My parents were not one way at home and another way at church. They were the same people and they taught us the right way. They showed us the right way and then they just prayed for us. You know when the Lord got ready for us. When he called, we knew his voice because they taught us well.

Six months after revealing my secret, I accepted Jesus Christ into my life.

I would love to tell you that as soon as I accepted Christ into my life, I put porn down and never picked it up again. But the fact that the Lord would be patient enough with me, knowing that it did not take five minutes to get into it, it probably was not going to take five minutes to get out. But if I just walk with him, he will start shedding layers of bondage, abuse, molestation, no self-esteem, people pleasing. As I begin to walk, stuff started to fall off of me and that he would give me relationships. When God really wants to love you, he loves you through people. He brought people into my life to literally love all that crap out of me. It has been a great walk, 14 years still walking. It has been good! So, I do not carry secrets anymore.

Tim R

Never too Young *by Gustavo G*

I grew up always hanging around with my dad, who struggled with drinking. Everywhere he went I was right by his side; it was usually with his friends. Because of all the things I saw and was subject to, I developed an anger problem at the age of four. One of the saddest memories I have is my mom telling me that I was going to go to hell; I was only five years old! So there I was four, five, six years old relying on alcohol to get me through the day and cover the pain I felt at such a young age. I drank the majority of my life till I was thirty-three years old. The addiction started out with me being allowed to drink beer when I was with my dad, then as the years went by and I was growing older, it progressed to a six-pack, then it went to a twelve -pack, then an eighteen-pack, then finally a case of beer almost every day by the time I was in my twenties. I realized that after a while it was not enough, so I started drinking tequila mixed with Coke on the weekends, which turned into straight tequila. It got so bad that I started drinking bottle after bottle of tequila each day of the week. I drank to cover up all the pain I was feeling as that young boy and was trying not to think any more about life. I just wanted to hide the misery in my life! I wanted to forget everything that I had been through and was going through; a dad who really was not there for me, a mom who said I was going to go to hell, three failed marriages, the loss of four stillborn babies, and a car accident that almost took my life. I even had alcohol poisoning on three different occasions that almost took my life. I was not trying to kill myself, but through all these years I contemplated suicide many times. Because of the progression of the addiction, at the age of twenty-nine I found myself getting involved in illegal activity.

At thirty-two I was facing a conviction of forty-plus years in prison and would be ordered to pay restitution of a quarter million dollars because of the path I chose to take.

Then it happened, in July of 2011, I was going to end it all. I posted my plans on my Facebook page by bidding everyone farewells and as soon as it posted the comments blew up, my text messages blew up, my phone kept ringing from people calling me. It was the first time I really felt loved! One friend who called said to me, "You need to pray" and I said, "Pray, what is that? I have never done that before," and she said, "Just talk to God and cry out to him." I was at work at the time, so I went out to the car, and for exactly one hour, I prayed whatever came to mind. When I was done, I felt different, I felt relieved, I felt forgiven and felt all this weight that I carried was taken off my shoulders. August of 2011, I made the decision to make Jesus the Lord of my life, and soon afterwards I got baptized. I said to myself that I was going to start living right, no more doing wrong, no more alcohol, no more women, no more bars/clubs, no more of the crazy life that I was living. A few weeks later I was right back to the old life because trying to live a Godly life, trying to live right was not easy. Trying to go from drinking one day to not drinking the next without guidance was extremely hard. I did not know how to do it, so I came to realize that the God way was not for me because the alcoholic life was all that I knew.

October of 2013 my son's mom introduced me to Gateway Church. From the day that I stepped in the front door, it felt like home. When Pastor Robert started speaking it was about everything that was going on in my life. I thought to myself, "Who told him about me? How did he know to preach about this? Someone must have told him that I was coming." I would love to tell you that from that day on I have never drank again, but I cannot. I struggled with the addiction a while longer. Even though my life was nothing like it was before stepping into the church, I still continued to drink some beer until one day when I finally got the revelation that I am no longer an alcoholic. I have not stopped attending Gateway Church since that first day, and I thank God for this church and all the pastors. I stopped doing all the crooked stuff which has made my life easier. I now serve as an usher and attend the North Fort Worth campus on weekly basis.

July of 2014, I went on an event put on by Fellowship of the Sword called Quest for five and half days to spend time on a ranch seeking after the heart of God. At the ranch God said, "Gustavo, you are not my son." I replied, "Look at everything I am doing up to this point." And He said, "It is not about what you do, it is about your heart." God opened my eyes to so many things that I had hidden deep in my heart, some I knew and some things I did not know were there. I was finally getting set free and understanding what God had meant. On the last night, God told me, "Now you are my son" and from then on, my life changed forever. Since I changed my life, I serve God seven days a week, day, and night. Anywhere that I can serve, whether at church or in the streets I do. I share my testimony on the streets with people that I meet; I go to different churches and share it with men's groups and youth groups as well. God changed my life and rescued me from death, and I am eternally grateful.

I am now free from the alcohol addiction that held me captive for so many years. I am no longer facing any criminal charges from the companies that were after me and they are no longer seeking restitution. Only God can have done this for me, and he can work miracles in your life as well.

Gustavo G.

The Open Door *by Alex L.*

One morning, as my mom is rushing out the door to get to work, she kneels down to give me a kiss and says good-bye. "I love you, baby, I'll see you when I get home from work," she says. I'm screaming, crying, and yelling, "Mommy, don't go. Please don't leave me." As I look back and relive that moment, the first thing that I feel is pain. I remember being so young and trying to process everything that had just happened.

My first sexual encounter was at the age of three. While my parents were at work, my babysitter attempted sexual intercourse with me. In addition, she abused me in other ways, so much so, that I was terrified to be left alone with her. I eventually built up the courage to tell my parents that "my pee pee hurts." The babysitter did not realize it at the time, but she had an occurring yeast infection, which she had passed on to me. As a result, I contracted an infection that required surgery on my genital opening. I remember that moment and the surgery as clearly as the day it had happened; the pain from the surgery was everlasting. I remember the confusion, the misunderstanding of why things were happening to me the way they were after the surgery. I remember saying "Mommy, Daddy it hurts, make it go away!" That is where this journey started for me. At a young age, a desire and urge had been awakened before its time, which later on in life gave birth to a very addictive personality and opened doors that led to sexual immorality, pornography, drugs, and alcohol.

Years went by and life took its course. The older I got, the more I forced myself to forget about what had happened. But the thing is the more I forced myself to forget, the worse my addictive mentality got. The desire to escape that feeling of fear and shame grew so strong that I found myself experimenting with anything to feel comfortable with in my own skin. At age thirteen I tried my first cigarette. Not too much longer I tried smoking marijuana for the first time. My curiosity for anything that would make me feel better got stronger and stronger. The desire to feel better grew so strong and intense that I began to be immoral with women uncontrollably and started using heavier drugs. All these drugs used to help me temporarily escape the reality of what I started to feel at the age of three; shame, guilt, and the feeling of unworthiness. I just was not able to look at myself the way I wanted to, and the more I tried, the more I was not able to. I could not bear to look at myself for who I was on the inside. I did what I could to numb myself on the outside with drugs, alcohol, and women so that I could cover up what I was feeling on the inside. I thought that is the way God looked at me and I could not help to feel rejected and not loved.

I lived a life feeling completely trapped and confined. My life consisted of me avoiding anything that was uncomfortable to me, anything to feel good and not bad. My desire for anything to mask what I was feeling outside of my comfort zone was uncontrollable. Drugs, drinking, and women controlled who I was but not who I wanted to be. My addictive personality had complete control of my life, so much that all my choices in life were based on how I felt at that exact moment. And if it was not what I liked; I ran to anything to make me feel better. Finally one day, I made a choice and reacted immediately upon what I felt at that moment, which was fear. I got into a fight, and it involved more than one person. I was charged that night with aggravated assault with a deadly weapon. I was eighteen when I was charged with a second-degree felony. At twenty -one I went to trial by Judge, open plea and was convicted and sentenced to six years in the Texas Department of Criminal Justice. When this happened, I did not know how to process what I had just heard. I did not know where to begin with what had just happened, and most of all I did not know how to deal with the fact that I was twenty-one years old and about to spend six years of my life behind bars, away from family and loved ones.

It took years for me to recognize and accept that the Lord loved me so much that he allowed me to be sentenced just long enough to feel the things that I had been running from my entire life. Not everyone is going to think the way I did at that moment. It is so easy for us to see our lives through the filter of our brokenness in the midst of a life-altering situation like mine. It is difficult to see the good in a bad situation, let alone not see it through our own perspective but Gods. I thought to myself, my entire life I have avoided anything and everything that has caused me the slightest pain. Who am I to run from anything that hurts, to hide behind a bottle, a drug, or a woman to numb the pain! When Jesus went to the cross willingly and laid his life down for me so that I would not perish but have everlasting life. I said, "God, if this is your will for my life then so be it. If I have to suffer a little while to go on then to share in your glory, then count me in. I love you and I know you love me, and you are faithful!" At that moment I knew that the current situation I was going through would not last forever. Yes, it was not easy, and at times so painful to the point that I did suffer a tremendous amount of emotional pain. But if I had not gone through what I had gone through in prison from an emotional, physical, and spiritual standpoint, I would not have been able to experience what God has for me today. I remember feeling so ashamed because of who I was, where I had been and what I had done. Society has a way of placing this stamp on you as a failure when you are a convicted felon.

For the first time in my life I was sober long enough to feel what I now know with no shadow of a doubt to be the Holy Spirits warm hands of grace on my shoulders. And that day it was like he said, "Alex, you need to let me tell you what I think about you for once." He began to place things on my heart that no person could ever do because of where I was, in prison. He put me in a place where no man could reach me the way he can. Words of affirmation began pouring out, "Alex, you are redeemed, a new creation, called and anointed. And you know why? Because your mine, not based on your perfect track record, or your ability to get it right, you are mine solely because of the blood of Jesus and you need to see yourself the way that I see you, as my son!" That was the beginning of something new in my life. I wish I could tell you that I waved some magic wand along with saying some magic words then all of sudden I was a new person. That is not what happened; it took me twenty-one years to get to prison and it has taken years for me to truly be free. I had to be patient with myself along with knowing that the Lord would be patient enough with me, understanding that in due time, layers of bondage, abuse, shame, and those chains from prison would begin to fall off. Salvation is a journey! Today I am on staff at Gateway Church, and I get to tell people about who I was, where I have been, and who I am now.

Alex L.

Section 3

Helpful Scriptures, Parables and Prayers

This subject matter index is not meant to be exhaustive. This is only a few of the many topics you need to know and may feel as well as scriptures found throughout the guidebook.

Scriptures

Accountability:

Brothers, if anyone is caught in any transgression, you who are spiritual should restore him in a spirit of gentleness. Keep watch on yourself, lest you too be tempted. Bear one another's burdens, and so fulfill the law of Christ. For if anyone thinks he is something, when he is nothing, he deceives himself. But let each one test his own work, and then his reason to boast will be in himself alone and not in his neighbor. For each will have to bear his own load. (Galatians 6:1–5, ESV)

Iron sharpens iron, and one man sharpens another. (Proverbs 27:17, ESV)

So then each of us shall give account of himself to God. (Romans 14:12)

Therefore comfort each other and edify one another, just as you also are doing. (1 Thessalonians 5:11)

I fed you with milk, not solid food, for you were not yet strong enough [to be ready for it]; but even yet you are not strong enough [to be ready for it], For you are still [unspiritual, having the nature] of the flesh [under the control of ordinary impulses]. For as long as [there are] envying and jealousy and wrangling and factions among you, are you not unspiritual and of the flesh, behaving yourselves after a human standard and like mere (unchanged) men? For when one says, I belong to Paul, and another, I belong to Apollos, are you not [proving yourselves] ordinary (unchanged) men? (1 Corinthians 3:2–4, AMP)

Anger:

In your anger do not sin": Do not let the sun go down while you are still angry, and do not give the devil a foothold. He who has been stealing must steal no longer, but must work, doing something useful with his own hands, that he may have something to share with those in need. Do not let any unwholesome talk come out of your mouths, but only what is helpful for building others up according to their needs, that it may benefit those who listen. Get rid of all bitterness, rage, and anger, brawling and slander, along with every form of malice. (Ephesians 4:26–29,31, NIV)

My dear brothers and sisters, take note of this: Everyone should be quick to listen, slow to speak and slow to become angry, for man's anger does not bring about the righteous life that God desires. (James 1:19–20, NIV)

A fool vents all his feelings, But a wise man holds them back. (Proverbs 29:11)

A gentle answer turns away wrath, but a harsh word stirs up anger. (Proverbs 15:1, NIV)

Refrain from anger and turn from wrath; do not fret—it leads only to evil. For those who are evil will be destroyed, but those who hope in the Lord will inherit the land. (Psalm 37:8–9, NIV)

But I say to you that whoever is angry with his brother without a cause shall be in danger of the judgment. And whoever says to his brother, "Raca!" shall be in danger of the council. But whoever says, "You fool!" shall be in danger of hell fire. (Matthew 5:22)

Baby Dedication:

Then she made a vow and said, "O Lord of hosts, if You will indeed look on the affliction of Your maidservant and remember me, and not forget Your maidservant, but will give Your maidservant a male child, then I will give him to the Lord all the days of his life, and no razor shall come upon his head." (1 Samuel 1:11)

Train up a child in the way he should go, And when he is old he will not depart from it. (Proverbs 22:6)

Baptism:

Therefore we were buried with Him through baptism into death, that just as Christ was raised from the dead by the glory of the Father, even so we also should walk in newness of life. (Romans 6:4)

Jesus answered, "Most assuredly, I say to you, unless one is born of water and the Spirit, he cannot enter the kingdom of God." (John 3:5)

Go therefore and make disciples of all the nations, baptizing them in the name of the Father and of the Son and of the Holy Spirit. (Matthew 28:19)

Then those who gladly received his word were baptized; and that day about three thousand souls were added to them. (Acts 2:41)

He who believes and is baptized will be saved; but he who does not believe will be condemned. (Mark 16:16)

Belief:

Today in the town of David a Savior has been born to you; he is the Messiah, the Lord. (Luke 2:11, NIV)

For, He has put all things under His feet." But when He says "all things are put under Him," it is evident that He who put all things under Him is excepted. (1 Corinthians 15:26)

But without faith it is impossible to please Him, for he who comes to God must believe that He is, and that He is a rewarder of those who diligently seek Him. (Hebrews 11:6)

He who believes and is baptized will be saved; but he who does not believe will be condemned. (Mark 16:16)

We are assured and know that [God being a partner in their labor] all things work together and are [fitting into a plan] for good to and for those who love God and are called according to [His] design and purpose. For those whom He foreknew [of whom He was aware and loved beforehand], He also destined from the beginning [foreordaining them] to be molded into the image of His Son [and share inwardly His likeness], that He might become the firstborn among many brethren. (Romans 8:28–29, AMP)

I am the vine, you are the branches. He who abides in Me, and I in him, bears much fruit; for without Me you can do nothing. (John 15:5)

Bondage:

Jesus answered them, Verily, verily, I say unto you, Every one that committeth sin is the bondservant of sin. (John 8:34, ASV)

For you did not receive the spirit of bondage again to fear, but you received the Spirit of adoption by whom we cry out, "Abba, Father." (Romans 8:15)

I am the Lord your God, who brought you out of Egypt, out of the land of slavery. (Exodus 20:2, NIV)

Now the Lord is the Spirit, and where the Spirit of the Lord is, there is freedom. (2 Corinthians 3:17, NIV)

And deliver all those who through fear of death were subject to lifelong slavery. (Hebrews 2:15)

I will be found by you, says the Lord, and I will bring you back from your captivity; I will gather you from all the nations and from all the places where I have driven you, says the Lord, and I will bring you to the place from which I cause you to be carried away captive. (Jeremiah 29:14)

Born Again:

Having been born again, not of corruptible seed but incorruptible, through the word of God which lives and abides forever. (1 Peter 1:23)

But as many as received Him, to them He gave the right to become children of God, to those who believe in His name. (John 1:12)

Therefore, if anyone is in Christ, he is a new creation; old things have passed away; behold, all things have become new. (2 Corinthians 5:17)

That if you confess with your mouth the Lord Jesus and believe in your heart that God has raised Him from the dead, you will be saved. For with the heart one believes unto righteousness, and with the mouth confession is made unto salvation. (Romans 10:9–10)

Jesus answered him, I assure you, most solemnly I tell you, that unless a person is born again (anew, from above), he cannot ever see (know, be acquainted with, and experience) the kingdom of God. Nicodemus said to Him, How can a man be born when he is old? Can he enter his mother's womb again and be born? Jesus answered, I assure you, most solemnly I tell you, unless a man is born of water and [even] the Spirit, he cannot [ever] enter the kingdom of God. What is born of [from] the flesh is flesh [of the physical is physical]; and what is born of the Spirit is spirit. Marvel not [do not be surprised, astonished] at My telling you, You must all be born anew (from above). (John 3:3–7, AMP)

Deliverance:

When the righteous cry for help, the Lord hears and delivers them out of all their troubles. (Psalm 34:17, ESV)

Then they cried to the Lord in their trouble, and he delivered them from their distress. (Psalm 107:6, ESV)

He said, "The Lord is my rock and my fortress and my deliverer. (2 Samuel 22:2, ESV)

And call upon me in the day of trouble; I will deliver you, and you shall glorify me. (Psalm 50:15, ESV)

And you will know the truth, and the truth will set you free. (John 8:32, ESV)

Flee from sexual immorality. Every other sin a person commits is outside the body, but the sexually immoral person sins against his own body. (1 Corinthians 6:18, ESV)

Depression:

Anxiety in the heart of man causes depression, But a good word makes it glad. (Proverbs 12:25)

The Lord also will be a refuge for the oppressed, A refuge in times of trouble. (Psalms 9:9)

Wait on the Lord; Be of good courage, And He shall strengthen your heart; Wait, I say, on the Lord! (Psalm 27:14)

Casting all your care upon Him, for He cares for you. (1 Peter 5:7)

Be anxious for nothing, but in everything by prayer and supplication, with thanksgiving, let your requests be made known to God; and the peace of God, which surpasses all understanding, will guard your hearts and minds through Christ Jesus. (Philippians 4:6–7)

Disease:

Who forgives all your iniquities, Who heals all your diseases. (Psalm 103:3)

And thus He fulfilled what was spoken by the prophet Isaiah, He Himself took [in order to carry away] our weaknesses and infirmities and bore away our diseases. (Matthew 8:17, AMP)

For an angel of the Lord went down at appointed seasons into the pool and moved and stirred up the water; whoever then first, after the stirring up of the water, stepped in was cured of whatever disease with which he was afflicted. (John 5:4, AMP)

At that very time Jesus cured many who had diseases, sicknesses and evil spirits, and gave sight to many who were blind. (Luke 7:21, NIV)

And Jesus went throughout all the cities and villages, teaching in their synagogues and proclaiming the gospel of the kingdom and healing every disease and every affliction. (Matthew 9:35, ASV)

Then His fame went throughout all Syria; and they brought to Him all sick people who were afflicted with various diseases and torments, and those who were demon-possessed, epileptics, and paralytics; and He healed them. (Matthew 4:24)

Emotional Stress:

For God has not given us a spirit of fear, but of power and of love and of a sound mind. (2 Timothy 1:7)

Peace I leave with you, My peace I give to you; not as the world gives do I give to you. Let not your heart be troubled, neither let it be afraid. (John 14:27)

And my God shall supply all your need according to His riches in glory by Christ Jesus. (Philippians 4:19)

Blessed be the God and Father of our Lord Jesus Christ, the Father of sympathy (pity and mercy) and the God [Who is the Source] of every comfort (consolation and encouragement), Who comforts (consoles and encourages) us in every trouble (calamity and affliction), so that we may also be able to comfort (console and encourage) those who are in any kind of trouble or distress, with the comfort (consolation and encouragement) with which we ourselves are comforted (consoled and encouraged) by God. (2 Corinthians 1:3–4, AMP)

Faith:

Be on your guard; stand firm in the faith; be men of courage; be strong. (1 Corinthians 16:13, NIV)

I have fought the good fight, I have finished the race, I have kept the faith. (2 Timothy 4:7, NIV)

If you have faith as small as a mustard seed, you can say to this mulberry tree, "Be pulled up by the roots, and be planted in the sea," and it will obey you. (Luke 17:5–6, AMP)

Now faith is the substance of things hoped for, the evidence of things not seen. (Hebrews 11:1)

But without faith it is impossible to please Him, for he who comes to God must believe that He is, and that He is a rewarder of those who diligently seek Him. (Hebrews 11:6)

So then faith comes by hearing and hearing by the word of God. (Romans 10:17)

For we walk by faith, not by sight. (2 Corinthians 5:7)

Favor:

May the favor of the Lord our God rest on us; establish the work of our hands for us—yes, establish the work of our hands. (Psalm 90:17, NIV)

My son do not forget my teaching, but let your heart keep my commandments, for length of days and years of life and peace they will add to you. Let not steadfast love and faithfulness forsake you; bind them around your neck; write them on the tablet of your heart. So you will find favor and good success in the sight of God and man. (Proverbs 3:1–4, ESV)

For you bless the righteous, O Lord; you cover him with favor as with a shield. (Psalm 5:12, ESV)

And Jesus increased in wisdom and in stature and in favor with God and man. (Luke 2:52, ESV)

Toward the scorners he is scornful, but to the humble he gives favor. (Proverbs 3:34, ESV)

So Joseph found favor in his sight and attended him, and he made him overseer of his house and put him in charge of all that he had. (Genesis 39:4, ESV)

So brace up your minds; be sober (circumspect, morally alert); set your hope wholly and unchangeably on the grace (divine favor) that is coming to you when Jesus Christ (the Messiah) is revealed. (1 Peter 1:13, AMP)

But God, who is rich in mercy, because of His great love with which He loved us, even when we were dead in trespasses, made us alive together with Christ (by grace you have been saved), and raised us up together, and made us sit together in the heavenly places in Christ Jesus, that in the ages to come He might show the exceeding riches of His grace in His kindness toward us in Christ Jesus. For by grace you have been saved through faith, and that not of yourselves; it is the gift of God, not of works, lest anyone should boast. (Ephesians 2:4–9)

Fear:

The fear of the Lord is the beginning of wisdom, And the knowledge of the Holy One is understanding. (Proverbs 9:10)

The Lord is my light and my salvation; Whom shall I fear? The Lord is the strength of my life; Of whom shall I be afraid? (Psalm 27:1)

When I am afraid, I put my trust in you. In God, whose word I praise—in God I trust and am not afraid. What can mere mortals do to me? (Psalm 56:3–4, NIV)

So do not fear, for I am with you; do not be dismayed, for I am your God. I will strengthen you and help you; I will uphold you with my righteous right hand. (Isaiah 41:10, NIV)

For I am the Lord, your God, who takes hold of your right hand and says to you, Do not fear; I will help you. (Isaiah 41:13, NIV)

Do not fear, for you will not be ashamed; Neither be disgraced, for you will not be put to shame; For you will forget the shame of your youth, And will not remember the reproach of your widowhood anymore. (Isaiah 54:4)

For God has not given us a spirit of fear, but of power and of love and of a sound mind. (2 Timothy 1:7)

There is no fear in love. But perfect love drives out fear, because fear has to do with punishment. The one who fears is not made perfect in love. (1 John 4:18, NIV)

Be strong and of good courage, do not fear nor be afraid of them; for the Lord your God, He is the One who goes with you. He will not leave you nor forsake you. (Deuteronomy 31:6)

Forgiven/ Forgiveness:

Then He said to her, "Your sins are forgiven." (Luke 7:48)

And whenever you stand praying, forgive, if you have anything against anyone, so that your Father also who is in heaven may forgive you your trespasses. (Mark 11:25, ESV)

He says, "Forgive, and you will be forgiven." (Luke 6:37, NIV)

For if you forgive other people when they sin against you, your heavenly Father will also forgive you. But, if you do not forgive others their sins, your Father will not forgive your sins. (Matthew 6:14–15, NIV)

Be kind to one another, tenderhearted, forgiving one another, as God in Christ forgave you. (Ephesians 4:32, ESV)

Therefore if you bring your gift to the altar, and there remember that your brother has something against you, leave your gift there before the altar, and go your way. First be reconciled to your brother, and then come and offer your gift. (Matthew 5:23–24)

Grace:

And He said to me, My grace is sufficient for you, for My strength is made perfect in weakness. Therefore most gladly I will rather boast in my infirmities, that the power of Christ may rest upon me. (2 Corinthians 12:9)

But may the God of all grace, who called us to His eternal glory by Christ Jesus, after you have suffered a while, perfect, establish, strengthen, and settle you. (1 Peter 5:10)

Being justified freely by His grace through the redemption that is in Christ Jesus. (Romans 3:24)

In Him we have redemption through His blood, the forgiveness of sins, according to the riches of His grace. (Ephesians 1:7)

But by the grace of God I am what I am, and His grace toward me was not in vain; but I labored more abundantly than they all, yet not I, but the grace of God which was with me. (1 Corinthians 15:10)

For you know the grace of our Lord Jesus Christ, that though He was rich, yet for your sakes He became poor, that you through His poverty might become rich. (2 Corinthians 8:9)

And God is able to make all grace abound toward you, that you, always having all sufficiency in all things, may have an abundance for every good work. (2 Corinthians 9:8)

So brace up your minds; be sober (circumspect, morally alert); set your hope wholly and unchangeably on the grace (divine favor) that is coming to you when Jesus Christ (the Messiah) is revealed. (1 Peter 1:13, AMP)

But God, who is rich in mercy, because of His great love with which He loved us, even when we were dead in trespasses, made us alive together with Christ (by grace you have been saved), and raised us up together, and made us sit together in the heavenly places in Christ Jesus, that in the ages to come He might show the exceeding riches of His grace in His kindness toward us in Christ Jesus. For by grace you have been saved through faith, and that not of yourselves; it is the gift of God, not of works, lest anyone should boast. (Ephesians 2:4–9)

Let us then approach God's throne of grace with confidence, so that we may receive mercy and find grace to help us in our time of need. (Hebrews 4:16)

Healing:

And immediately they left the boat and their father and followed Him. And Jesus went about all Galilee, teaching in their synagogues, preaching the gospel of the kingdom, and healing all kinds of sickness and all kinds of disease among the people. Then His fame went throughout all Syria; and they brought to Him all sick people who were afflicted with various diseases and torments, and those who were demon-possessed, epileptics, and paralytics; and He healed them. (Matthew 4:22–24)

Surely, He has borne our griefs And carried our sorrows; Yet we esteemed Him stricken, Smitten by God, and afflicted. But he was wounded for our transgressions, he was bruised for our iniquities; the chastisement of our peace was upon him; and with his stripes we are healed. (Isaiah 53:4–5, ASV)

Confess your trespasses to one another, and pray for one another, that you may be healed. The effective, fervent prayer of a righteous man avails much. (James 5:16)

And when the sun was setting, all they that had any sick with divers diseases brought them unto him; and he laid his hands on every one of them, and healed them. (Luke 4:40, ASV)

But so much the more went abroad the report concerning him: and great multitudes came together to hear, and to be healed of their infirmities. (Luke 5:15, ASV)

And a woman having an issue of blood twelve years, who had spent all her living upon physicians, and could not be healed of any. (Luke 8:43, ASV)

Who his own self bare our sins in his body upon the tree, that we, having died unto sins, might live unto righteousness; by whose stripes ye were healed. (1 Peter 2:24, ASV)

O Jehovah my God, I cried unto thee, and thou hast healed me. (Psalms 30:2, ASV)

He sent His word and healed them, And delivered them from their destructions. (Psalm 107:20)

Heal me, O Lord, and I shall be healed; Save me, and I shall be saved, For You are my praise. (Jeremiah 17:14)

Then your light shall break forth like the morning, Your healing shall spring forth speedily, And your righteousness shall go before you; The glory of the Lord shall be your rear guard. (Isaiah 58:8)

Behold, I will bring it health and healing; I will heal them and reveal to them the abundance of peace and truth. (Jeremiah 33:6)

Then Jesus went about all the cities and villages, teaching in their synagogues, preaching the gospel of the kingdom, and healing every sickness and every disease among the people. (Matthew 9:35)

But when the multitudes knew it, they followed Him; and He received them and spoke to them about the kingdom of God, and healed those who had need of healing. (Luke 9:11)

How God anointed Jesus of Nazareth with the Holy Spirit and with power, who went about doing good and healing all who were oppressed by the devil, for God was with Him. (Acts 10:38)

Hope:

Be strong, and let your heart take courage, All ye that hope in Jehovah. (Psalm 31:24, ASV)

Behold, the eye of Jehovah is upon them that fear him, Upon them that hope in his lovingkindness. (Psalms 38:18, ASV)

For in thee, O Jehovah, do I hope: Thou wilt answer, O Lord my God. (Psalms 38:15, ASV)

Hope deferred makes the heart sick, But when the desire comes, it is a tree of life. (Proverbs 13:12)

The wicked is banished in his wickedness, But the righteous has a refuge in his death. (Proverbs 14:32)

Remember my affliction and roaming, The wormwood and the gall. My soul still remembers and sinks within me. This I recall to my mind, Therefore I have hope. (Lamentations 3:19–21)

So brace up your minds; be sober (circumspect, morally alert); set your hope wholly and unchangeably on the grace (divine favor) that is coming to you when Jesus Christ (the Messiah) is revealed. (1 Peter 1:13, AMP)

Hostile:

The mind governed by the flesh is hostile to God; it does not submit to God's law, nor can it do so. (Romans 8:7, NIV)

If in spite of these things you do not accept my correction but continue to be hostile toward me, I myself will be hostile toward you and will afflict you for your sins seven times over. (Leviticus 26:23–24, NIV)

Humility:

For whoever exalts himself will be humbled, and he who humbles himself will be exalted. (Luke 14:11)

Therefore humble yourselves under the mighty hand of God, that He may exalt you in due time. (1 Peter 5:6)

By humility and the fear of the Lord Are riches and honor and life. (Proverbs 22:4)

I'll never forget the trouble, the utter lostness, the taste of ashes, the poison I've swallowed. I remember it all—oh, how well I remember—the feeling of hitting the bottom. But there's one other thing I remember, and remembering, I keep a grip on hope. (Lamentations 3:19–21)

Humble yourselves in the sight of the Lord, and He will lift you up. (James 4:10)

Judging:

Judge not, that you be not judged. For with the judgment you pronounce you will be judged, and with the measure you use it will be measured to you. Why do you see the speck that is in your brother's eye, but do not notice the log that is in your own eye? Or how can you say to your brother, 'Let me take the speck out of your eye,' when there is the log in your own eye? You hypocrite, first take the log out of your own eye, and then you will see clearly to take the speck out of your brother's eye. (Matthew 7:1–5, ESV)

Judge not, and you will not be judged; condemn not, and you will not be condemned; forgive, and you will be forgiven. (Luke 6:37, ESV)

Therefore let us not judge one another anymore, but rather resolve this, not to put a stumbling block or a cause to fall in our brother's way. (Romans 14:13)

Kindness:

The Spirit of the Lord God is upon me, because the Lord has anointed and qualified me to preach the Gospel of good tidings to the meek, the poor, and afflicted; He has sent me to bind up and heal the brokenhearted, to proclaim liberty to the [physical and spiritual] captives and the opening of the prison and of the eyes to those who are bound, To proclaim the acceptable year of the Lord [the year of His favor] and the day of vengeance of our God, to comfort all who mourn. (Isaiah 61:1–2, AMP)

But God, who is rich in mercy, because of His great love with which He loved us, even when we were dead in trespasses, made us alive together with Christ (by grace you have been saved), and raised us up together, and made us sit together in the heavenly places in Christ Jesus, that in the ages to come He might show the exceeding riches of His grace in His kindness toward us in Christ Jesus. For by grace you have been saved through faith, and that not of yourselves; it is the gift of God, not of works, lest anyone should boast. (Ephesians 2:4–9)

And let us consider one another in order to stir up love and good works. Not forsaking the assembling of ourselves together, as is the manner of some, but exhorting one another, and so much the more as you see the day approaching. (Hebrews 10:24–25)

Love:

You have heard that it was said, "You shall love your neighbor and hate your enemy." But I say to you, love your enemies, bless those who curse you, do good to those who hate you, and pray for those who spitefully use you and persecute you, that you may be sons of your Father in heaven; for He makes His sun rise on the evil and on the good, and sends rain on the just and on the unjust. (Matthew 5:43–45)

Above all things have intense and unfailing love for one another, for love covers a multitude of sins [forgives and disregards the offenses of others]. (1 Peter 4:8, AMP)

And you shall love the Lord your God with all your heart, with all your soul, with all your mind, and with all your strength.' This is the first commandment. And the second, like it, is this: 'You shall love your neighbor as yourself.' There is no other commandment greater than these. (Mark 12:30–31)

A new commandment I give to you, that you love one another; as I have loved you, that you also love one another. By this all will know that you are My disciples, if you have love for one another. (John 13:34–35)

If you [really] love Me, you will keep (obey) My commands. (John 14:15, AMP)

Whoever has my commands and keeps them is the one who loves me. The one who loves me will be loved by my Father, and I too will love them and show myself to them. (John 14:21, NIV)

For God so loved the world that He gave His only begotten Son, that whoever believes in Him should not perish but have everlasting life. (John 3:16)

Greater love has no one than this: to lay down one's life for one's friends. (John 15:13)

Mercy:

Therefore know that the Lord your God, He is God, the faithful God who keeps covenant and mercy for a thousand generations with those who love Him and keep His commandments. (Deuteronomy 7:9)

Through the Lord's mercies we are not consumed, Because His compassions fail not. They are new every morning; Great is Your faithfulness. (Lamentations 3:22–23)

Therefore be merciful, just as your Father also is merciful. (Luke 6:36)

Blessed are the merciful, For they shall obtain mercy. (Matthew 5:7)

Blessed be the God and Father of our Lord Jesus Christ, the Father of sympathy (pity and mercy) and the God [Who is the Source] of every comfort (consolation and encouragement), Who comforts (consoles and encourages) us in every trouble (calamity and affliction), so that we may also be able to comfort (console and encourage) those who are in any kind of trouble or distress, with the comfort (consolation and encouragement) with which we ourselves are comforted (consoled and encouraged) by God. (2 Corinthians 1:3–4, AMP)

Let us then approach the throne of grace with confidence, so that we may receive mercy and find grace to help us in our time of need. (Hebrews 4:16)

Pain/Suffering:

[Healing for the Backslider] And one shall say, "Heap it up! Heap it up! Prepare the way, Take the stumbling block out of the way of My people." (Isaiah 57:14)

Let your conduct be without covetousness; be content with such things as you have. For He Himself has said, "I will never leave you nor forsake you. (Hebrews 13:5)

He also brought me up out of a horrible pit, Out of the miry clay, And set my feet upon a rock, And established my steps. (Psalm 40:2)

There has befallen them the thing spoken of in the true proverb. The dog turns back to his own vomit, and. The sow is washed only to wallow again in the mire. (2 Peter 2:22, AMP)

As a dog returns to his vomit, so a fool returns to his folly. (Proverbs 26:11, AMP)

Patience:

Be still, and know that I am God; will be exalted among the nations, I will be exalted in the earth! (Psalm 46:10)

But those who wait on the Lord Shall renew their strength; They shall mount up with wings like eagles, They shall run and not be weary, They shall walk and not faint. (Isaiah 40:31)

Therefore be patient, brethren, until the coming of the Lord. See how the farmer waits for the precious fruit of the earth, waiting patiently for it until it receives the early and latter rain. You also be patient. Establish your hearts, for the coming of the Lord is at hand. (James 5:7–8)

And let us not grow weary while doing good, for in due season we shall reap if we do not lose heart. (Galatians 6:9)

A person's wisdom yields patience; it is to one's glory to overlook an offense. (Proverbs 19:11, NIV)

If anyone will not welcome you or listen to your words, leave that home or town and shake the dust off your feet. (Matthew 10:14, NIV)

Perseverance:

But the one who endures to the end will be saved. (Matthew 24:13, ESV)

And let us not grow weary of doing good, for in due season we will reap, if we do not give up. (Galatians 6:9, ESV)

Count it all joy, my brothers, when you meet trials of various kinds, for you know that the testing of your faith produces steadfastness. And let steadfastness have its full effect, that you may be perfect and complete, lacking in nothing. (James 1:2–4, ESV)

Blessed is the man who remains steadfast under trial, for when he has stood the test he will receive the crown of life, which God has promised to those who love him. (James 1:12, ESV)

Prayer:

And when he came to the place, he said to them, pray that you may not [at all] enter into temptation. And he withdrew from them about a stone's throw and knelt down and prayed, saying Father, if you are willing, remove this cup from me; yet not my will, but yours be done. And there appeared to him an angel from heaven, strengthening him in spirit. And being in an agony [of mind], he prayed [all the] more earnestly and intently, and sweat became like great clots of blood dropping down upon the ground. (Luke 22:40–44, AMP)

If My people who are called by My name will humble themselves, and pray and seek My face, and turn from their wicked ways, then I will hear from heaven, and will forgive their sin and heal their land. (2 Chronicles 7:14)

Confess your trespasses to one another, and pray for one another, that you may be healed. The effective, fervent prayer of a righteous man avails much. (James 5:16)

And whatever you ask in My name, that I will do, that the Father may be glorified in the Son. If you ask anything in My name, I will do it. (John 14:13–14)

Our Father in heaven, Hallowed be your name. Your kingdom come. Your will be done on earth as it is in heaven. Give us this day our daily bread. And forgive us our debts, As we forgive our debtors. And do not lead us into temptation, but deliver us from the evil one. For Yours is the kingdom and the power and the glory forever. Amen! (Matthew 6:9–13)

Finally, be strong in the Lord and in his mighty power. Put on the full armor of God, so that you can take your stand against the devil's schemes. For our struggle is not against flesh and blood, but against the rulers, against the authorities, against the powers of this dark world and against the spiritual forces of evil in the heavenly realms. Therefore put on the full armor of God, so that when the day of evil comes, you may be able to stand your ground, and after you have done everything, to stand. Stand firm then, with the belt of truth buckled around your waist, with the breastplate of righteousness in place, and with your feet fitted with the readiness that comes from the gospel of peace. In addition to all this, take up the shield of faith, with which you can extinguish all the flaming arrows of the evil one. Take the helmet of salvation and the sword of the Spirit, which is the word of God. And pray in the Spirit on all occasions with all kinds of prayers and requests. With this in mind, be alert and always keep on praying for all the Lord's people. Pray also for me, that whenever I speak, words may be given me so that I will fearlessly make known the mystery of the gospel, for which I am an ambassador in chains. Pray that I may declare it fearlessly, as I should. (Ephesians 6:10–20, NIV)

Enter into His gates with thanksgiving, And into His courts with praise. Be thankful to Him, and bless His name. (Psalm 100:4)

Repent:

Repent, then, and turn to God, so that your sins may be wiped out, that times of refreshing may come from the Lord. (Acts 3:19, NIV)

Then Peter said to them, "Repent, and let every one of you be baptized in the name of Jesus Christ for the remission of sins; and you shall receive the gift of the Holy Spirit. (Acts 2:38)

From that time Jesus began to preach and to say, "Repent, for the kingdom of heaven is at hand." (Matthew 4:17)

Salvation:

Most assuredly, I say to you, he who does not enter the sheepfold by the door, but climbs up some other way, the same is a thief and a robber. But he who enters by the door is the shepherd of the sheep. To him the doorkeeper opens, and the sheep hear his voice; and he calls his own sheep by name and leads them out. And when he brings out his own sheep, he goes before them; and the sheep follow him, for they know his voice. (John 10:1–4)

Jesus said to him, "I am the way, the truth, and the life. No one comes to the Father except through Me." (John 14:6)

So, friends, we can now—without hesitation—walk right up to God, into "the Holy Place." Jesus has cleared the way by the blood of his sacrifice, acting as our priest before God. The "curtain" into God's presence is his body. (Hebrews 10:20, MSG)

Heal me, O Lord, and I shall be healed; Save me, and I shall be saved, For You are my praise. (Jeremiah 17:14)

Therefore, if anyone is in Christ, he is a new creation; old things have passed away; behold, all things have become new. (2 Corinthians 5:17)

That if you confess with your mouth the Lord Jesus and believe in your heart that God has raised Him from the dead, you will be saved. For with the heart one believes unto righteousness, and with the mouth confession is made unto salvation. (Romans 10:9–10)

For God so greatly loved and dearly prized the world that He [even] gave up His only begotten (unique) Son, so that whoever believes in (trusts in, clings to, relies on) Him shall not perish (come to destruction, be lost) but have eternal (everlasting) life. (John 3:16, AMP)

And he said to me, "Do not seal the words of the prophecy of this book, for the time is at hand. He who is unjust, let him be unjust still; he who is filthy, let him be filthy still; he who is righteous, let him be righteous still; he who is holy, let him be holy still. And behold, I am coming quickly, and My reward is with Me, to give to everyone according to his work. I am the Alpha and the Omega, the Beginning and the End, the First and the Last. Blessed are those who do His commandments, that they may have the right to the tree of life, and may enter through the gates into the city. But outside are dogs and sorcerers and sexually immoral and murderers and idolaters, and whoever loves and practices a lie. I, Jesus, have sent My angel to testify to you these things in the churches. I am the Root and the Offspring of David, the Bright and Morning Star." (Revelation 22:10–16)

Ho! Everyone who thirsts, Come to the waters; And you who have no money, Come, buy and eat. Yes, come, buy wine and milk Without money and without price. (Isaiah 55:1)

For the wages of sin is death, but the gift of God is eternal life in Christ Jesus our Lord. (Romans 6:23)

Self-Pity:

Blessed be the God and Father of our Lord Jesus Christ, the Father of sympathy (pity and mercy) and the God [Who is the Source] of every comfort (consolation and encouragement), Who comforts (consoles and encourages) us in every trouble (calamity and affliction), so that we may also be able to comfort (console and encourage) those who are in any kind of trouble or distress, with the comfort (consolation and encouragement) with which we ourselves are comforted (consoled and encouraged) by God. (2 Corinthians 1:3–4, AMP)

Shame:

Do not fear, for you will not be ashamed; Neither be disgraced, for you will not be put to shame; For you will forget the shame of your youth, And will not remember the reproach of your widowhood anymore. (Isaiah 54:4)

As Scripture says, Anyone who believes in him will never be put to shame. (Romans 10:11, NIV)

Keep vigilant watch over your heart; that's where life starts. Don't talk out of both sides of your mouth; avoid careless banter, white lies, and gossip. Keep your eyes straight ahead; ignore all sideshow distractions. Watch your step, and the road will stretch out smooth before you. Look neither right nor left; leave evil in the dust. (Proverbs 4:25, MSG)

Sickness (see Healing):

Sin:

For the wages of sin is death, but the gift of God is eternal life in Christ Jesus our Lord. (Romans 6:23)

For all have sinned and fall short of the glory of God. (Romans 3:23, NIV)

If we say that we have not sinned, we make him a liar, and his word is not in us. (1 John 1:10, ASV)

No one who is born of God will continue to sin, because God's seed remains in them; they cannot go on sinning, because they have been born of God. (1 John 3:9, NIV)

If we confess our sins, he is faithful and just and will forgive us our sins and purify us from all unrighteousness. (1 John 1:9, NIV)

But if we walk in the light as He is in the light, we have fellowship with one another, and the blood of Jesus Christ His Son cleanses us from all sin. (1 John 1:7)

And said, Truly I say to you, unless you repent (change, turn about) and become like little children [trusting, lowly, loving, forgiving], you can never enter the kingdom of heaven [at all]. (Matthew 18:3, AMP)

Surrender:

Set your mind on things above, not on things on the earth. (Colossians 3:2)

Delight yourself in the Lord, and he will give you the desire of your heart. Commit your ways to the Lord, trust in him, and he will act. He will bring forth your righteousness as the light, and your justice as the noonday. (Psalms 37:4–6, ESV)

Then he said to them all: Whoever wants to be my disciple must deny themselves and take up their cross daily and follow me. (Luke 9:23, NIV)

Tongue:

Death and life are in the power of the tongue, and those who love it will eat its fruits. (Proverbs 18:21, ESV)

Whoever desires to love life and see good days, let him keep his tongue from evil and his lips from speaking deceit. (1 Peter 3:10, ESV)

A soft answer turns away wrath, but a harsh word stirs up anger. (Proverbs 15:1, ESV)

And the tongue is a fire, a world of unrighteousness. The tongue is set among our members, staining the whole body, setting on fire the entire course of life, and set on fire by hell. (James 3:6, ESV)

But what comes out of the mouth proceeds from the heart, and this defiles a person. For out of the heart come evil thoughts, murder, adultery, sexual immorality, theft, false witness, slander. (Matthew 15:18–19, ESV)

Trust:

It is better to take refuge in the Lord than to trust in humans. (Psalms 118:8, NIV)

And I am convinced and sure of this very thing, that He Who began a good work in you will continue until the day of Jesus Christ [right up to the time of His return], developing [that good work] and perfecting and bringing it to full completion in you. (Philippians 1:6, AMP)

Trust in the Lord with all your heart, and lean not on your own understanding; In all of your ways acknowledge him, and he will direct your paths. (Proverbs 3:5–6)

Unrighteousness:

If we confess our sins, he is faithful and just to forgive us our sins and to cleanse us from all unrighteousness. (1 John 1:9, ESV)

For the wrath of God is revealed from heaven against all ungodliness and unrighteousness of men, who suppress the truth in unrighteousness, because what may be known of God is manifest in them, for God has shown it to them. For since the creation of the world His invisible attributes are clearly seen, being understood by the things that are made, even His eternal power and Godhead, so that they are without excuse, because, although they knew God, they did not glorify Him as God, nor were thankful, but became futile in their thoughts, and their foolish hearts were darkened. Professing to be wise, they became fools, and changed the glory of the incorruptible God into an image made like corruptible man—and birds and four-footed animals and creeping things. (Romans 1:18–32)

Vision/Revelation:

He answered and said to them, "Because it has been given to you to know the mysteries of the kingdom of heaven, but to them it has not been given. (Matthew 13:11)

Where there is no vision [no redemptive revelation of God], the people perish; but he who keeps the law [of God, which includes that of man]—blessed (happy, fortunate, and enviable) is he. (Proverbs 29:18, AMP)

And afterward I will pour out My Spirit upon all flesh; and your sons and your daughters shall prophesy, your old men shall dream dreams, your young men shall see visions. (Joel 2:28, AMP)

And the Lord answered me and said, Write the vision and engrave it so plainly upon tablets that everyone who passes may [be able to] read [it easily and quickly] as he hastens by. (Habakkuk 2:2, AMP)

For the vision is yet for an appointed time and it hastens to the end [fulfillment]; it will not deceive or disappoint. Though it tarry, wait [earnestly] for it, because it will surely come; it will not be behindhand on its appointed day. (Habakkuk 2:3, AMP)

Once You spoke in a vision to Your devoted ones and said, I have endowed one who is mighty [a hero, giving him the power to help—to be a champion for Israel]; I have exalted one chosen from among the people. (Psalm 89:19, AMP)

For God [does reveal His will; He] speaks not only once, but more than once, even though men do not regard it [including you, Job]. (Job 33:14, AMP)

And He said, Hear now My words: If there is a prophet among you, I the Lord make Myself known to him in a vision and speak to him in a dream. (Numbers 12:6, AMP)

Now there was in Damascus a disciple named Ananias. The Lord said to him in a vision, Ananias. And he answered, Here am I, Lord. And the Lord said to him, Get up and go to the street called Straight and ask at the house of Judas for a man of Tarsus named Saul, for behold, he is praying [there]. (Acts 9:10–11, AMP)

And the Father Who sent Me has Himself testified concerning Me. Not one of you has ever given ear to His voice or seen His form (His face—what He is like). [You have always been deaf to His voice and blind to the vision of Him.] (John 5:37, AMP)

Now the boy Samuel ministered to the Lord before Eli. The word of the Lord was rare and precious in those days; there was no frequent or widely spread vision. (1 Samuel 3:1, AMP)

Now the people kept waiting for Zachariah, and they wondered at his delaying [so long] in the sanctuary. But when he did come out, he was unable to speak to them; and they [clearly] perceived that he had seen a vision in the sanctuary; and he kept making signs to them, still he remained dumb. (Luke 1:21–22, AMP)

And moreover, some women of our company astounded us and drove us out of our senses. They were at the tomb early [in the morning] but did not find His body; and they returned saying that they had [even] seen a vision of angels, who said that He was alive! (Luke 24:22–23, AMP)

[There] a vision appeared to Paul in the night: a man from Macedonia stood pleading with him and saying, Come over to Macedonia and help us! (Acts 16:9, AMP)

Beloved, do not imitate evil, but imitate good. He who does good is of God; he who does evil has not seen (discerned or experienced) God [has enjoyed no vision of Him and does not know Him at all]. (3 John 1:11, AMP)

[This is] the revelation of Jesus Christ [His unveiling of the divine mysteries]. God gave it to Him to disclose and make known to His bond servants certain things which must shortly and speedily come to pass in their entirety. And He sent and communicated it through His angel (messenger) to His bond servant John, who has testified to and vouched for all that he saw [in his visions], the word of God and the testimony of Jesus Christ. (Revelation 1:1–2, AMP)

I was in the Spirit [rapt in His power] on the Lord's Day, and I heard behind me a great voice like the calling of a war trumpet, saying, I am the Alpha and the Omega, the First and the Last. Write promptly what you see (your vision) in a book and send it to the seven churches which are in Asia—to Ephesus and to Smyrna and to Pergamum and to Thyatira and to Sardis and to Philadelphia and to Laodicea. (Revelation 1:10–11, AMP)

It was the Lord's pleasure for His righteousness' sake [in accordance with a steadfast and consistent purpose] to magnify instruction and revelation and glorify them. (Isaiah 42:21, AMP)

Now to Him Who is able to strengthen you in the faith which is in accordance with my Gospel and the preaching of (concerning) Jesus Christ (the Messiah), according to the revelation (the unveiling) of the mystery of the plan of redemption which was kept in silence and secret for long ages. (Romans 16:25, AMP)

But the natural, nonspiritual man does not accept or welcome or admit into his heart the gifts and teachings and revelations of the Spirit of God, for they are folly (meaningless nonsense) to him; and he is incapable of knowing them [of progressively recognizing, understanding, and becoming better acquainted with them] because they are spiritually discerned and estimated and appreciated. (1 Corinthians 2:14, AMP)

For I want you to know, brethren, that the Gospel which was proclaimed and made known by me is not man's gospel [a human invention, according to or patterned after any human standard]. For indeed I did not receive it from man, nor was I taught it, but [it came to me] through a [direct] revelation [given] by Jesus Christ (the Messiah). (Galatians 1:11–12, AMP)

[For I always pray to] the God of our Lord Jesus Christ, the Father of glory, that He may grant you a spirit of wisdom and revelation [of insight into mysteries and secrets] in the [deep and intimate] knowledge of Him. (Ephesians 1:17, AMP)

Do not spurn the gifts and utterances of the prophets [do not depreciate prophetic revelations nor despise inspired instruction or exhortation or warning]. (1 Thessalonians 5:20, AMP)

Yet I am writing you a new commandment, which is true (is realized) in Him and in you, because the darkness (moral blindness) is clearing away and the true Light (the revelation of God in Christ) is already shining. (1 John 2:8, AMP)

Wickedness:

How then can I do this great wickedness, and sin against God? (Genesis 39:9)

That you put off, concerning your former conduct, the old man which grows corrupt according to the deceitful lusts, and be renewed in the spirit of your mind, and that you put on the new man which was created according to God, in true righteousness and holiness. Therefore, putting away lying, "Let each one of you speak truth with his neighbor," for we are members of one another. "Be angry, and do not sin": do not let the sun go down on your wrath, nor give place to the devil. Let him who stole steal no longer, but rather let him labor, working with his hands what is good, that he may have something to give him who has need. Let no corrupt word proceed out of your mouth, but what is good for necessary edification, that it may impart grace to the hearers. And do not grieve the Holy Spirit of God, by whom you were sealed for the day of redemption. Let all bitterness, wrath, anger, clamor, and evil speaking be put away from you, with all malice. And be kind to one another, tenderhearted, forgiving one another, even as God in Christ forgave you. (Ephesians 4:22–32)

For a day in Your courts is better than a thousand. I would rather be a doorkeeper in the house of my God Than dwell in the tents of wickedness. (Psalms 84:10)

Wisdom:

Give, and it will be given to you. Good measure, pressed down, shaken together, running over, will be put into your lap. For with the measure you use it will be measured back to you. (Luke 6:38, ESV)

Do not be conformed to this world (this age), [fashioned after and adapted to its external, superficial customs], but be transformed (changed) by the [entire] renewal of your mind [by its new ideals and its new attitude], so that you may prove [for yourselves] what is the good and acceptable and perfect will of God, even the thing which is good and acceptable and perfect [in His sight for you]. (Romans 12:2, AMP)

Here is another version:

And do not be conformed to this world, but be transformed by the renewing of your mind, that you may prove what is that good and acceptable and perfect will of God. (Romans 12:2)

Do not be unequally yoked together with unbelievers. For what fellowship has righteousness with lawlessness? And what communion has light with darkness? (2 Corinthians 6:14)

Worry:

So then, banish anxiety from your heart and cast off the troubles of your body, for youth and vigor are meaningless. (Ecclesiastes 11:10, NIV)

And my God shall supply all your need according to His riches in glory by Christ Jesus. (Philippians 4:19)

Therefore I say to you, do not worry about your life, what you will eat or what you will drink; nor about your body, what you will put on. Is not life more than food and the body more than clothing? (Matthew 6:25)

Worship:

God is Spirit, and those who worship Him must worship in spirit and truth. (John 4:24)

Give to the Lord the glory due to His name; worship the Lord in the beauty of holiness or in holy array. (Psalm 29:2, AMP)

Oh come, let us worship and bow down; Let us kneel before the Lord our Maker. (Psalm 95:6)

Exalt the Lord our God, And worship at His footstool—He is holy. (Psalm 99:5)

Draw near to God and He will draw near to you. Cleanse your hands, you sinners; and purify your hearts, you double-minded. (James 4:8)

Worthy are You, our Lord and God, to receive the glory and the honor and dominion, for You created all things; by Your will they were [brought into being] and were created. (Revelation 4:11, AMP)

Parables

The Parable of the Rich Fool

Then one from the crowd said to Him, "Teacher, tell my brother to divide the inheritance with me." But He said to him, "Man, who made Me a judge or an arbitrator over you?" And He said to them, "Take heed and beware of covetousness, for one's life does not consist in the abundance of the things he possesses." Then He spoke a parable to them, saying: "The ground of a certain rich man yielded plentifully. And he thought within himself, saying, 'What shall I do, since I have no room to store my crops?' So he said, 'I will do this: I will pull down my barns and build greater, and there I will store all my crops and my goods. And I will say to my soul, "Soul, you have many goods laid up for many years; take your ease; eat, drink, and be merry." But God said to him, 'Fool! This night your soul will be required of you; then whose will those things be which you have provided?' "So is he who lays up treasure for himself, and is not rich toward God." (Luke 12:13–21)

The Parable of the Unmerciful Servant

Then Peter came to Jesus and asked, "Lord, how many times shall I forgive my brother or sister who sins against me? Up to seven times? Jesus answered, "I tell you, not seven times, but seventy-seven times. Therefore, the kingdom o heaven is like a king who wanted to settle accounts with his servants. As he began the settlement, a man who owed him ten thousand bags of gold was brought to him. Since he was not able to pay, the master ordered that he and his wife and his children and all that he had be sold to repay the debt. At this the servant fell on his knees before him. 'Be patient with me,' he begged, 'and I will pay back everything.' The servant's master took pity on him, canceled the debt and let him go. But when that servant went out, he found one of his fellow servants who owed him a hundred silver coins. He grabbed him and began to choke him. 'Pay back what you owe me!' he demanded. His fellow servant fell to his knees and begged him, 'Be patient with me, and I will pay it back.' But he refused. Instead, he went off and had the man thrown into prison until he could pay the debt. When the other servants saw what had happened, they were outraged and went and told their master everything that had happened. Then the master called the servant in. 'You wicked servant,' he said, 'I canceled all that debt of yours because you begged me to. Shouldn't you have had mercy on your fellow servant just as I had on you?' In anger his master handed him over to the jailers to be tortured, until he should pay back all he owed. This is how my heavenly Father will treat each of you unless you forgive your brother or sister from your heart. (Matthew 18:21–35, NIV)

Prayers

Salvation

Dear God in heaven, I come to you in the name of Jesus. I acknowledge to you and myself that I am a sinner, and I am sorry for my sins and the life that I have lived. I need your forgiveness to be in my life. Father, I know I cannot get rid of this addiction alone. Only you and you alone can take it from me and deliver me. I surrender my will over to you and ask that you make me clean as snow, like you did with so many others. Give me the same power they have seen so I too can see clearly. I believe that your only begotten son, Jesus Christ, shed his precious blood on the cross at Calvary and died for my sins, and I am now willing to turn from my sin. You said in, Romans 10:9, that if we confess the Lord our God and believe in our hearts that God raised Jesus from the dead, we shall be saved. Right now, I confess Jesus as the Lord of my soul. With my heart, I believe that God raised Jesus from the dead. I accept Jesus Christ as my own personal savior, and according to your word, right now, I am saved. I thank you God, for your unlimited grace given to me by Jesus. I thank you that your grace always leads to repentance. Therefore I ask that, through the work of Jesus, you transform my life right now so that I may bring glory and honor to you alone and not to myself. I thank you for giving me eternal life. I thank you for your mercy, even when I was not aware of it. I ask and give permission to the Holy Spirit to lead the way. Amen!

Repenting

Father God, according to 1 John 1:9, I confess (speak out the sin here) and ask you for your forgiveness to purify my soul and cleanse me from unrighteousness. I am sorry God, that I allowed this filth to rule and reign over my life. I declare with my mouth that (speak out the sin here) will no longer have procession or control over my life. I take this sin and lay it at the foot of the cross where Jesus now has control over it. I thank you Father, for the Holy Spirit, who lives inside me, to help me overcome this area. Amen!

Asking for Forgiveness

Lord, please forgive me for what I have done to you and myself. I offer up this forgiveness prayer in hopes that you will look at my mistakes no more. I know that what I did was wrong and against your word, but I hope that you will forgive me just as you forgave others like me. I will try Lord to change. I will make every attempt to not give in to temptation again. I know that you are the most important thing in my life right now. I ask for your guidance to help me overcome the shame and guilt I placed on myself and allowing others to dictate my future. I forgive myself for all of my wrongs. I know that I am not a bad person and will go easy on myself. Bless me Lord. Amen!

Hurt List

Father, I ask you for help with my hurt list. Help me to remember all the people I have hurt and the offense that caused that hurt. Help me to remember how I felt at that moment. Help me not to be afraid of bringing up these feelings but to know that you are near to love me and comfort me with the pain. I ask this in Jesus's name. Amen!

Sample Prayer

Father God, thank you for this day. Thank you that I get to enter into your court with an open heart and an open mind. Thank you for loving me and sending your son to die on the cross so I may live. I praise your holy name. I thank you for loving me enough to not let me die. I am sorry I did not believe in you when they told me about you years ago. I was only looking at the things of this world and not on the things in heaven. I can see that you are who they say you are. I can feel your never-ending love in my heart. I can see your true existence throughout your word and on this earth. I yield myself to the Holy Spirit to show me where I went wrong and how to correct it. What to say and when not to say anything. I love you God, and may my hope be built on nothing less than Jesus's blood and his righteousness. Amen!

Lord's Prayer:

Our Father in heaven,
Hallowed be Your name.
Your kingdom come.
Your will be done On earth as it is in heaven.
Give us this day our daily bread.
And forgive us our debts, As we forgive our debtors. And do not lead us into temptation, But deliver us from the evil one.
For Yours is the kingdom and the power and the glory forever. Amen!
(Matthew 6:9–13)

PRAY—Praise, Repent, Acknowledge, Yield

About the Author

Anthony Ordille was born in Hammonton, New Jersey to a truck driver and a stay-at-home mom, along with three brothers and two sisters. After attending Catholic school, he finished out his high school years at a public school where he graduated in 1976. In Mr. Ordille's teen years he walked away from serving God and became rebellious, hateful, and was on a destructive path doing things that he is not proud of.

At the age of fifteen Ordille experienced getting drunk on beer for the first time. One day after school he was at the neighbor's house playing around and they went downstairs to the basement to raid the refrigerator where the neighbor's dad kept his beer. After the first three bottles, he started feeling funny; his vision clouded and after a few more, felt no pain. One of the guys there lived downtown, and they decided to ride their bicycles to his house. They were giggling and having a hard time keeping their bicycles straight; almost getting hit by some passing cars. When they arrived, they staggered to the second floor of the garage, and it was not long before Anthony felt sick and vomited all over his friends' father's truck through a hole in the floor. Anthony swore he would never touch a beer again. He broke that promise to himself shortly afterwards.

Within the first year of high school, Ordille smoked his first joint. It made him choke at first but after a few more hits he felt funny. After some time, Anthony started to notice that it was not so bad and really enjoyed it. From then on, each time he got high, he noticed that the emotional pain he felt as a young kid was starting to be replaced with a different feeling, one that did not hurt, one that made him forget episodes that built up anger, resentment, and other emotions. When Anthony had asked someone about this feeling, they told him it makes everything easier to cope with. He began wondering if what they were telling him was true. How would it make him feel if he were to do more than just smoke weed? Anthony started drinking wine with classmates during school dances, being arrested once for disorderly conduct, but that did not make him stop. He got drunk at other school functions and other different activities becoming obnoxious.

Anthony had been working on the farm for some years at this point and summer was coming around, which meant he would be working long days, six to seven days a week for about three months. This is when other drugs started to be introduced to him, drugs that would help him stay up longer and work more without being tired; drugs like cocaine and black beauties (speed). He started buying weed by the pound, pills by the bag, and cocaine by the ounce. Anthony did this for years and found it was the only way he could work those long hours. After high school Ordille remained on the farm, using more drugs to help him wake up after a hard night and to get though the long days, and drinking during lunches.

There was a time when getting drugs was difficult so a friend of his and himself would stop at a hobby shop to buy model glue, cut it open, and squeeze it into a paper bag and huff it. It would make them lightheaded and was a nice substitute for the drugs. When Anthony got to the point that he wanted more drugs and could not afford them, he started dealing thinking it would be a good way to supply his habit. Mr. Ordille never made any money because he would consume all the profit, and sometimes did not sell any at all, he would just keep it because the habit demanded more. Anthony kept up this lifestyle for years and most people around him never even knew it.

During high school, Mr. Ordille joined up with some guys that formed a rock 'n' roll band that started playing at school dances. Anthony began hanging out with them hooking up wires, carrying equipment in and out of the truck and working the lights/soundboard when they would play. They started playing at other functions like parties, weddings, bars, and this was starting to get exciting. There was a song for this part of life, "Sex, and Drugs and Rock 'n' Roll". Anthony loved it and could not wait for the end of the week to come because most of their gigs were on the weekends. During this time, he started letting his hair grow longer, and by the time he decided to get a haircut, it was past his shoulder blades.

Anthony spent a lot of time with these guys during those years and was enjoying this lifestyle because the whole time he would be with them, he would not be thinking about how sad he felt about his past. As time went by, the band members went in different directions, and one of the guitar players joined with some other guys who were going to write their own music. Since Anthony was close to this guy, he went with him which took his life to a whole new level. They would go to the Philadelphia area during the week for practice and then play gigs on the weekends, sometimes in other states. Ordille said, "This was the life: partying, getting high all the time and playing at night clubs for all the free beer I could drink". Anthony's official title was "Roadie" and even has his name on an album, titled, "911". Even though he did not play an instrument he said that working with the band was just as good; it was a fast pace, exciting, out-of-this-world experience, and he loved it!

After the band stopped playing, he was in his mid-twenties and continued with the bar lifestyle for a number of years. He even joined a carnival for a season working their way up the east coast to Canada and then back down to finish the season in Macon, Georgia.

In fact, Mr. Ordille was living a life filled with alcohol, drugs, lying, cheating, stealing, adulterous acts, rock-n-roll, basically a destructive lifestyle. Throughout the more than sixteen years of this type of living some of the choice of drugs were: marijuana, speed, smoking crack, cocaine, shooting heroin and just about anything else in between. Drinking beer and hard liquor sometimes from the time he got up to the time he passed out, days on end. There were times that Anthony wanted to just go to sleep and never wake up. This almost came true at the age of thirty-two when one night he just had enough and decided to take his own life. God had other plans and would not allow it to happen. So, when Ordille saw that he was in trouble he ran to his family for help.

That night was the end of his misery and started a whole new chapter in his life. After going through a detox in the fall of 1989, his family brought him to a Rehab Center, Riverside House in Philadelphia, Pennsylvania, where he spent the next thirty days learning about who he was. As he was in rehabilitation, he saw the poem "Footprints in the Sand" hanging on the wall and thought to himself that all those years he was away from God, walking by himself, what a waste of time. One day as he was reading the poem, he asked God for forgiveness and heard God say, "Anthony, it was not your prints in the sand walking alone but mine carrying you". When Ordille told God some years back that he did not want nothing to do with him, God knew that he did not mean it, therefore God never left him. That was when he turned his life back towards God and the creator of Heaven and Earth was forgiving and merciful.

After getting out of the rehab Ordille went right to Alcoholics Anonymous and Narcotics Anonymous meetings and became involved in both organizations for five years; speaking at meetings, jails, and other institutions, holding various positions. Within those five years he knew that there was more to life than just working and going to meetings, so he started to get less involved. It was a few years later when Mr. Ordille's lifestyle started to change. He started to hang more and more around the bar for lunch and people who drank and one weekend he started to drink again. Only a beer here and there but it became comfortable. The weekends started to be filled with drinking at the camping grounds, until one day his life fell apart.

Ten years after being in the Rehab Anthony found himself back in a position that he never thought would happen. Even though he did not get back into drugs he noticed his drinking was starting to get out of control and his wife at that time seen it too and left him. He knew that Jesus Christ had to become first in his life. That is when, in October of 1998, Mr. Ordille had decided to accept Jesus as Lord of his life with the help of his nephew.

Mr. Ordille started going to church right after he got saved and joined the choir and was a sound board operator for a short time. He did whatever was needed to be done; like clean up after a food drive, or youth dance, etcetera. After a couple of years Anthony started attending a church on Sunday nights, which became his full-time church for the next four years. He was asked to join the worship team, and even was asked by the pastor to work by his side during ministry at times and was part of the state-wide prayer ministry for New Jersey.

Within that time Anthony Ordille had taken a job with Sam's Club as a night stocker. Within three months became Personnel Manager and within nine months was promoted into management. That position led them to move to two other States. In Exton, Pennsylvania, Anthony took a home study course from the World Harvest Bible College External Studies located out of Columbus, Ohio, and would get involved with a local church as much as the job would let him. During his years at Sam's Club, he had made the market field his service to God by evangelizing inside the walls, this was great when he was a Personnel Manager, and they would come to him for prayer and direction. After being relocated to Victoria, Texas Mr. Ordille left that job to relocate to the Fort Worth, Texas area to pursue ministry. After getting settled in, the Ordille family join a local church where he got involved with the men's group, prayer, and took part in some other areas of ministry within the two years they attended.

Even though the ministry doors did not open for Mr. Ordille at that time, he became certified as a Therapon Belief Therapist (CBT) with The Therapon Institute Texas location. Completed the Associate Degree Program of Christian Studies with a 3.8 (ACS), The Bachelor Degree Program in Church Ministry with a 3.9 (BCh.M) and has completed all his certification to be a Licensed Minister through The Sure Foundation Fellowship.

In the summer of 2010, the Ordille family started to attend Gateway Church in Southlake, Texas and that fall they became members. Jumping right into volunteering; Anthony joined the usher team and in January 2012 was asked to be a captain. June of that year was asked to be overseer at one of the new campuses, Fort Worth Campus, and January of 2013 was invited to apply for the Deacon Ministry. On March 18, 2013 was ordained in the Deacon Ministry.

Furthering the mission field, In the spring of 2013 Anthony Ordille published his first book about his life, "An Injection of Faith-One Addicts Journey to Deliverance", In the process of this book being read by people all across the land, and testimonies on how much it changed their lives, Ordille decided to publish a second book in 2016,"12 Steps to an Addictive Free Live", along with a workbook that will be worked as a 12-step program with God and his son Jesus being the higher power that delivers all addictions.

So in conclusion, after twenty-two years Mr. Anthony Ordille is here testifying the love of God and how his son Jesus died for our sins. He has put God first in everything he does, and God has given him a new life. One without the pain he felt as a child. A life without the desire to drink, smoke cigarettes, or do drugs of any kind, no matter what curve ball life throws his way.

Anthony's hope to every reader, and those that choose to work the 12-step program, is that through his life experiences, all who are struggling with addictions will find the truth, follow his lead to a life of hope, peace, and forgiveness, and that their addiction, no matter what it may be, will not run their lives any longer.

Are you on the road to freedom?

Contact Information

Addictive Free Life is based in United States of America

Send all inquiries through website at:
www.anthonyordille.com/

Copies of this book may be purchased at:
www.amazon.com
www.barnesandnoble.com/

If you would like to purchase bulk orders for meetings, please contact AFL through our website.

To order the workbook, please visit any of the websites above.

Endnotes

❖ Chapter 1: Do I Belong Here

[1] *Merriam-Webster's Collegiate Dictionary*, "By permission. From *Merriam-Webster's Collegiate® Dictionary*, 11th Edition ©2015 by Merriam-Webster, Inc. (www. Merriam-Webster.com)."

[2] *Webster's Dictionary of the English Language*, Based on *The Random House Dictionary*, Classic Edition, copyright © 1983 by Random House, Inc., All rights reserved, pp. 10.

[3] *Merriam-Webster's Collegiate Dictionary*, "By permission. From *Merriam-Webster's Collegiate® Dictionary*, 11th Edition ©2015 by Merriam-Webster, Inc. (www. Merriam-Webster.com)."

❖ Chapter 2: Is There Hope for Me?

[1] http://www.iamsecond.com/seconds/tim-ross/, Tim Ross's Testimony, iamsecond.com is the website from the I Am Second movement, Dallas-Ft. Worth, Texas, Used by permission from Tim Ross, accessed April 19, 2015.

❖ Chapter 3: Stepping into Faith

[1] Webster's New World Dictionary, Third College Edition, © 1988 by Simon & Schuster, Inc., pp. 487.

❖ Chapter 4: Putting Your Faith into Action: Steps 1-12

Step 3

[1] *Webster's Dictionary of the English Language*, Based on *The Random House Dictionary*, Classic Edition, copyright © 1983 by Random House, Inc., All rights reserved, pp. 802.

[2] Anthony Ordille, *An Injection of Faith: One Addict's Journey to Deliverance*, 2013, pp. 117–124.

Step 4

[1] Crystal Maria Scott (2014-06-06). *Sin and the Church: Perspectives and Principles for Powerful Christian Living* (Kindle Location 13). AuthorHouse. Kindle Edition, pp. 1622.

Step 5

[1] http://www.tentmaker.org/Quotes/forgivenessquotes. htm, Forgiveness Quotes, page one, Henry Ward Beecher, Tentmaker Ministries, Hermann, MO, © 2014, last accessed April 4, 2015.

Step 6

[1] *Merriam-Webster's Collegiate Dictionary*, "By permission. From *Merriam-Webster's Collegiate® Dictionary*, 11th Edition ©2015 by Merriam-Webster, Inc. (www. Merriam-Webster.com)."

[2] https://www.psychologytoday.com/blog/fulfillment- any-age/201208/the-definitive-guide-guilt, "The Definitive Guide to Guilt," Post published by Susan Krauss Whitbourne PhD on August 11, 2012, Psychology Today © 1991–2015 Sussex Publishers, LLC, last accessed April 11, 2015.

[3] http://www.therapists.com/fundamentals/guilt- shame, "Guilt and Shame," quoted by Beverly Engel cited by Therapists.com, Therapists.com is a division of Mir Internet Marketing Inc., Chicago, IL., © 2012–2014, last accessed February 12, 2015, Used by permission from Beverly Engel, beverlyengel.com.

Step 7

[1] *Webster's New World Dictionary,* Third College Edition, © 1988 by Simon & Schuster, Inc., pp. 1462.

Step 10

[1] http://www.godspy.co m/meditations/whoever wishes-to-come-after-me-must-deny-himself-take-up-his-cross-and-fol/, "Whoever wishes to come after me must deny himself, take up his cross, and follow me," By Admin, Posted 8/26/2008, Copyright © 2008 GODSPY.com | Published by Transmodern Media LLC, 1360 Park Lane, Pelham Manor, NY, last accessed April 7, 2015.

Step 11

[1] *Narcotics Anonymous*, Fifth Edition, Copyright ©.1988 by Narcotics Anonymous World Services, Inc., pp. 24.

Step 12

[1] *Webster's New World Dictionary*, Third College Edition, © 1988 by Simon & Schuster, Inc., pp. 498.

[2] *Merriam-Webster's Collegiate Dictionary*, "By permission. From *Merriam-Webster's Collegiate® Dictionary*, 11th Edition ©2015 by Merriam-Webster, Inc. (www. Merriam-Webster.com)."

[3] Excerpt taken from *How to Worship A King*, Zach Neese. Copyright © 2012 Gateway Create Publishing, pp. 60 & 62. Used by permission.

❖ Chapter 7: Recovery vs. Deliverance

[1] *Merriam-Webster's Collegiate Dictionary*, "By permission. From *Merriam-Webster's Collegiate® Dictionary*, 11th Edition ©2015 by Merriam-Webster, Inc. (www. Merriam-Webster.com)."

[2]*Webster's Dictionary of the English Language*, Based on *The Random House Dictionary*, Classic Edition, copyright © 1983 by Random House, Inc., All rights reserved, pp. 239.

❖ Chapter 8: Vision

[1] Anthony Ordille quote, http://anthonyordille.com /about-the-author/.

[2] *Merriam-Webster's Collegiate Dictionary*, "By permission. From *Merriam-Webster's Collegiate® Dictionary*, 11th Edition ©2015 by Merriam-Webster, Inc. (www. Merriam-Webster.com)."

Online source materials used as reference

http://www.glennobrien.net/Bible-copyright-information. html, Bible Copyright Information, Glenn O'Brien's website, accessed April 12, 2015.

https://prayerpowerministries.com/articles-on-prayer/, Prayer Articles "75 Timely Articles on Prayer—How to Pray," PrayerPower, Dallas, TX, accessed 05/4/2015